# THE POLITICAL ECONOMY OF A SOCIAL EUROPE

# The Political Economy of a Social Europe

## Understanding Labour Market Integration in the European Union

Michael F. Kluth

*Associate Professor of International Political Economy*
*Roskilde University*
*Denmark*

First published in Great Britain 1998 by
**MACMILLAN PRESS LTD**
Houndmills, Basingstoke, Hampshire RG21 6XS and London
Companies and representatives throughout the world

A catalogue record for this book is available from the British Library.

ISBN 0–333–73395–9

---

First published in the United States of America 1998 by
**ST. MARTIN'S PRESS, INC.,**
Scholarly and Reference Division,
175 Fifth Avenue, New York, N.Y. 10010

ISBN 0–312–21557–6

Library of Congress Cataloging-in-Publication Data
Kluth, Michael F.
The political economy of a social Europe : understanding labour
market integration in the European Union / Michael F. Kluth.
p.   cm.
Includes bibliographical references and index.
ISBN 0–312–21557–6 (cloth)
1. Labor market—European Union countries.   2. Labor policy–
–European Union countries.   3. European Union countries—Social
policy.   4. Europe—Economic integration.   I. Title.
HD5764.A6K63    1998
331.1'094—dc21
                                                                98–17439
                                                                    CIP

---

This book is printed on paper suitable for recycling and made from fully managed and
sustained forest sources.

10   9   8   7   6   5   4   3   2   1
07   06   05   04   03   02   01   00   99   98

Printed and bound in Great Britain by
Antony Rowe Ltd, Chippenham, Wiltshire

# Contents

# Preface

In 1993 a group of social scientists from the universities of Aalborg and Roskilde obtained a grant from the Danish Social Science Research Council.[1] Drawing on both economics, political science and cultural studies the group has spent three years exploring cross-disciplinary approaches to the issue of integration dynamics. This study is much indebted to these collective efforts. While the approach employed here does not reflect the theoretical preferences and positions of all group members, the joint research has been instrumental in identifying the key issues addressed in the conceptual framework which follows in the first chapter.

This book emanates from previous research on European labour market integration. In an earlier study I posed the question: why is a social dimension developing at the EU level? The inquiry looked at the policy process surrounding the adoption and the substance of key EU labour market policies.[2] Emphasis was on deliberate political attempts to develop EU labour market policy. While the original basis for EU labour market policy has been broadened by a series of European Court of Justice (ECJ) rulings, the study focused on the extension of scope brought about by bargaining and negotiation between various segments of the executive and legislative branches of supranational and national government and the social partners of the Union. In this contribution I attempt to develop and present a theoretical understanding of the dynamics of regional integration and apply it to the EU's Social Dimension.

The focus is on re-interpreting existing material rather than revealing new intriguing details about European level politicking. Ideally the presented framework is applicable to the full range of EU policy fields. Hence the purpose of this book is to present a theoretical construct for the analysis of the dynamics of regional integration, and illustrate its applicability to the case of the EU's social dimension.

Many people have greatly contributed to the present work. First and foremost the six other group members: Jesper Jespersen, Birgitte Gregersen, Staffan Zetterholm, Henrik Plasckhe, Björn Johnson and Bent Greve. The latter has served in the dual capacity as academic mentor, particularly in relation to the collection of the empirical material, and as head of my department he has shown considerable resilience in generously allowing me relief from teaching responsibilities thus greatly facilitating the making of this study.

Another Roskilde colleague, Professor Klaus Nielsen, has also been an important source of inspiration throughout the process as regards the momentous task of constructing theory. Professor John Zysman of Berkeley first spurred my interest for institutional political economy, for this I am extremely grateful.

Outside the realm of academia my friends in national and international bureaucracy have assisted me in focusing on the real world without losing track of the grander perspectives of societal change. I am greatly indebted to Jørn Andersen both as an ever encouraging friend and as co-author of various conference papers. In addition Søren Jakobsen has provided personal encouragement and substantial input. Both of them have willingly spent many evenings in endless academic discussions, generously sharing their experiences from the real world of bureaucratic policy making.

Last but not least I would like to express my deep gratitude to my wife Karen, who put up with me in the hectic months of writing. Although burdened by pregnancy leading to the delivery of a beautiful baby boy, she was always able to provide both moral support, inspiration and critical inputs. As an experienced economist having worked both as banker and investment consultant, she earnestly strived to rectify my overtly state-centred political science outlook.

Still, the idiosyncrasies, tautologies and downright errors critical readers undoubtedly will find in this book, are solely my responsibility. The book is dedicated to my two children Marie and Frederik.

# List of Abbreviations

| | |
|---|---|
| ANDIN | Andean Pact |
| ASEAN | Association of South-East Asian Countries |
| CAP | Common Agricultural Policy |
| CECE | European Committee of Construction Equipment Producers |
| CEEP | European Association of Public Enterprises |
| CEFIC | European Council of Chemical Manufacturers Federations |
| CEMA | European Manufacturers of Agricultural Machinery |
| CEN | European Technical Standards Committee |
| CENELEC | European Technical Standards Committee for Electrical Appliances |
| CEU | Commission of the European Union (see also EC) |
| CNPF | Leading French Employer Association |
| COMITEXTIL | Committee of Textile Industries |
| COPA | Committee of Professional Agricultural Organizations in the European Community |
| COREPER | Committee of Permanent Representatives |
| Council | The Council of Ministers |
| DG | Directorate General |
| DGV | Directorate General Number 5. In charge of Social and Labour Market Policy |
| EC | European Commission |
| ECJ | European Court of Justice |
| ECSC | European Coal and Steel Community |
| EEC | European Economic Community |
| EIPA | European Institute of Public Administration |
| EMU | Economic and Monetary Union |
| EO-WCL | European Organisation of the World Confederation of Labour |
| EP | European Parliament |
| EPC | European Political Cooperation |
| ERM | Exchange Rate Mechanism |
| ESC | Economic and Social Committee |
| ETUC | European Trade Union Confederation |

ix

| | |
|---|---|
| EU | European Union |
| EUFTU | European Confederation of Free Trade Unions |
| EUROCOTTON | Committee of Cotton Industries |
| EVCA | European Venture Capital Association |
| FEM | European Transport Material Producer Association |
| GATT | General Agreement on Trade and Tarifs (see also WTO) |
| IGC | Intergovernmental Conference |
| ILO | International Labour Organisation |
| LO | Scandinavian abbreviation for National Trade Union Center |
| MEP | Members of the European Parliament |
| MERCOSUR | Common Market of the Southern Cone |
| NAFTA | North American Free Trade Agreement |
| NIC | Newly Industrialized Countries |
| NTB | Non-Tariff Barriers |
| OECD | Organization for Economic Cooperation and Development |
| SAP | Social Action Programme |
| SCE | Standing Committee on Employment |
| SEA | Single European Act |
| SEM | Single European Market |
| SHCMOI | Safety and Health Commission for the Mining and Other Extractive Industries |
| SME | Small and Medium-sized Enterprises |
| SOP | Standard Operating Procedure |
| SOFAIS | French State-sponsored Venture Capital Insurance Scheme |
| TUTB | European Trade Union Technical Bureau for Health and Safety |
| TUC | Trade Union Congress |
| UK | United Kingdom |
| UNICE | Union of Industries in the European Community |
| WTO | World Trade Organisation (see also GATT) |

# 1 Introduction: Regional Integration and Political Economy

## 1 INTRODUCTION

Following the launch of the internal market scheme in the mid-eighties the world witnessed a resurgence in regional integrative ventures.[3] In Southeast Asia ASEAN gained a new momentum as it experienced a transformation from chiefly an intergovernmental venue created in response to security concerns towards a comprehensive regional trading bloc. In the Americas the United States took the lead in expanding a series of trading agreements with its northern neighbour to the NAFTA arrangement involving Mexico, USA and Canada. Further south the countries of Latin America have set up a number of regional trading systems the two most important being MERCOSUR and ANDIN (the Andean Pact).[4]

Regional integration is a key component in the globalisation process.[5] Understanding the dynamics of regional integration will shed important light on the overall dynamics of change in the world economy. Thus far, regional integration has mainly been analysed using static models coming out of either international trade theory (e.g. the works of Alan Winters and the Cechinni reports) or neo-realism as employed by political scientists (e.g. Andrew Moravcsik).[6]

In this book a theoretical framework capturing the dynamics of integration is explored. It rests on qualitative institutional political economy as associated with the new institutionalism of political science and sociology. In addition it incorporates elements of economic theories on technical change.

A theory pertaining to capture the dynamics of political developments is most appropriately tested against a highly volatile policy field. Hence the subject singled out for scrutiny is European level labour market policy. This particular field has gone through roller coaster-like ups and downs. Initially dwarfed by technocrats labour issues rose to prominence in the early seventies, some 15 years after the EU's inception. It suffered devastating defeat in the early eighties

1

only to reappear on the forefront of the European policy agenda in the wake of the internal market scheme and the subsequent institutional reforms.

## 1.1   Integration and Political Economy

The concept of integration has provoked extensive debate in political science and economics. Is it a 'process' or an 'end state', how may it be delineated from interdependence and which of the three basic dimensions – personal, relational and structural integration – should be emphasised. Should social integration be distinguished from assimilation and do personal, relational or structural integration result in the demise of previous personal traits, relational patterns and structural features? This study adopts the institutional stance and hence highlights the relational dimension.

Regional integration is thus defined as a process of cross-national, mutual adaptation of institutions in the spheres of state, market and civil society. Regional integration is a *process* with no absolute finality or fixed equilibrium. Integrating units be they state apparatuses, markets or civil societies, are themselves 'moving targets' as they continuously undergo processes of change. Integration constitutes a pattern of institutional change which subject all affected entities to roughly similar pressures which in turn provoke often strongly divergent responses.[7]

Regional integration evidently goes beyond the disciplinary boundaries of social science. As a minimum a political economy approach must be employed to unveil the dynamics of integrative processes.

There is no comprehensive theory on the political economy of regional integration. Such a theory must combine the insights of political science, economics and in addition incorporate the findings of other social and human sciences such as sociology, anthropology and cultural studies. In this study I set forth to explore the dynamics of European integration with a view to constructing a conceptual framework applicable on regional integration processes involving advanced economies.[8]

Political economy in no way constitutes a unified paradigm or approach to the study of societal processes and dynamics. While different traditions exist they are united in their aspiration to combine political and economic factors when accounting for societal dynamics.

At least three variances of political economy can be identified. First and foremost classical political economy, commonly associated with the works of David Ricardo but also including critics such as Karl Marx, was chiefly preoccupied with distributional issues.[9]

More contemporary, yet in theoretical contrast to classical thinkers, the public choice school offers a lucid yet philosophically restricted approach to political economy. In line with classical political economy, proponents of the public choice approach emphasise societal distribution mechanisms in their analysis. In terms of methodology, however, they differ sharply from the former. Essentially this branch of political economy applies the analytical tools of neoclassical economics on the study of political struggles over the authoritative distribution of values in society.

A third approach, which constitutes the vantage point of this study, has its origin in economic history and anthropology. Classical political economists like Smith and Ricardo, mainly focused on the distortive mechanisms of private and public regulatory regimes as based on the state and guild system. In the works of Friedrich List the focal point was on the possible positive effects on national economic performance of enhancing and re-engineering the properties of institutions deemed 'obstructive' by the liberalists, and employing them in the quest for industrialisation.[10] List implied that, contrary to liberalist beliefs, there are several paths to national economic success. Proponents of this brand of political economy thus argue along with Karl Polanyi that *markets, embedded in political and social institutions, are the creation of government and politics.* Polanyi vividly positions the economy vis-à-vis the political sphere as he observes that:

> [T]he market has been the outcome of a conscious and often violent intervention on the part of government which imposed the market organization on society for noneconomic ends.[11]

Institutional configurations thus not only hamper the operations of markets, they also define their future prospects and opportunities for development. As such, constraints and opportunities of national and regional economies are cast in with the associated institutional set-up. In a sense this brand of political economy ultimately argues the primacy of 'the political' over 'the economic'!

The dominant frame of political and economic activities has for the past few centuries been the nation state. Regional integration denotes a voluntary process of transgressing the nation state frame within the confinement of a distinct geography.

Hence a theory concerning the politics and economics of regional integration needs to address both the operation and dynamics of national and international systems. However, the initial framework of regional political cooperation has been the outcome of deliberate action of nation states, likewise the growth in regional and international transactions has been spurred by the relaxing of national economic control and the parallel erection of international economic regimes. These achievements are the outcome of deliberate state action informed by discourses advocating the political desirability of national and international trade liberalisation.

Consequently, a political economy of regional integration must take national systems as a point of departure. National frames for political practice and economic transaction are provided by institutions. Institutions are in turn the works of 'government and politics'. Government may be taken as a metaphor for state and politics as the societal processes determining state action.

Markets for money and labour provide the access point of politics in the economic sphere. Neither money nor labour can be characterised as commodities, but they nonetheless constitute two of the most important factor inputs of industrial economies.[12] Markets for money and labour are usually sheltered from immediate market pressures by means of vigorous regulations and intervention by government. As such they only conform marginally to the image of volatile exchange relations between traditionally optimising economic agents. Both markets are designed by 'government and politics' and consequently require explicit political analysis.

While markets for money and labour constitute a direct linkage between the 'economic' and the 'political' they are only two – albeit important – elements of national economic systems. Producers, distributors and vendors of manufactured goods constitute the backbone of industrial economies and are key users of labour and 'money' services. Viewed as a loose coalition in a power politics perspective, they are evidently able to aggregate demands to other segments of political economies as witnessed in relation to the EU's internal market scheme which is only now about to be matched with coherent money and labour components (respectively EMU and the Social Dimension).

In sum, three broad market components constitute economic systems: the labour market, the money market and the product market. The central point in the argument to come is that these markets entail specific social practices dictated by the character of the 'commodities' subject to transaction. Market specific social practices in turn implant particular biases on institutional design upon agents. Hence agents of money markets carry a set of institutional preferences which inform their action in power struggles on societal governance. Markets thus aggregate perceived ideals on institutional design and convey them to the 'sphere' of politics, shaping the settings within which they conduct their business.[13] Besides the three broad market categories outlined above, advanced economies also exhibit a state apparatus which likewise display an inherent set of preferences on institutional design stemming from social practices associated with the conduct of state governance. The state apparatus thus simultaneously constitutes the legitimate venue of antagonists, struggling in the political realm on issues of institutional design, and a complex structure subject to institutionalised patterns of behaviour while harbouring a distinct bias on market design and societal governance.

States, product, money and labour markets thus form the nucleus of political economies and consequently mark the entry point for an analysis of regional integration. The four pillars of political economies cannot, however, be analysed in isolation as they are highly interconnected.


## 2 STATES: ACTORS, INSTITUTIONS AND STRUCTURES

The dominant frame for political and economic activities has for the past few centuries been the nation state. As implied, nation states contain both the 'imagined community' of nation and a state apparatus.[14] Integration denotes the gradual joining of political structures (state apparatuses), civil societies (imagined communities) and markets across international boundaries. Market integration is the core purpose of regional endeavours such as the EU. Hence an institutional political economy of regional integration is initially concerned with how new regional markets are politically created on the basis of existing – often quite disparate – national markets.

States are commonly regarded as makers of institutions and in addition assigned the task of operating a wide range of regulatory arrangements. But while states usually possess the most comprehensive collection of power resources in nation states they are not sovereign in the true meaning of the word. This applies whether approached from a domestic or an international perspective. Although states are essential as both actors and structural frames with regard to societal dynamics they are themselves subject to the constraining and enabling sway of institutions.

Capturing the essence of the state has been a prime concern of social thought. While no longer as fashionable as in the seventies and early eighties, thinking about the state has been given new impetus with the advent of New Institutionalism which gained prominence in political science from the mid-eighties. This approach relinquished state theory from the structural strait and has helped to reinstate the importance of 'ideas' – as opposed to exogenous 'interests' – in both comparative and international government. Yet states and the societies in which they operate display structural features which need to be appreciated in political analysis. Similarly international relations are conducted in a global system where political and economic organisation matters.

International political economy identifies states as actors whereas traditional political economy, mainly focused on domestic issues, regards the state apparatus as a structural component. Social groupings, be they class-based, gender-based or occupational, may in turn be designated social actors in a national setting while students of international political economy would be more inclined to label them domestic structural components underpinning individual states.[15]

A conceptual framework operating with states as core features consequently needs to address the dual anchorage of the state as it operates in, and derives its legitimacy from, both a domestic and an international setting.[16] Such a framework must furthermore situate the state vis-à-vis the analytical categories of actor, institution and structure.

In the following I probe into the character of the state with a view to constructing an operational understanding of it which is simultaneously situated in domestic and international politics. While institutional analysis constitutes my vantage point it is attempted paired with a structural dimension taking into account common features of economically advanced societies. Unlike some of the writings by New Institutionalists my framework consequently does not pertain to have universal applicability.

Section 2.1 presents the dual anchorage of states. Making recourse to previous writings on the character of states, the restoration of ideas as a paramount feature in comparative government is emphasised in section 2.2 and associated sub-sections. In section 2.3 and accompanying sub-sections the exercise is repeated in connection with the field of international relations. Section 2.4 attempts to outline an understanding of states which draws on New Institutionalism. Finally the resultant state perception is positioned vis-à-vis markets.

## 2.1 The Dual Anchorage of the State

States have traditionally been treated as a nucleus of power in both comparative government and international relations. States interact on the international arena with other states. This is a key source of domestic legitimacy and power. However states rely on independent sources of domestic legitimacy and power in order to operate effectively on the international arena. States must, on the one hand, display a minimum level of societal autonomy and unity of action. At the same time, societal embeddedness and differentiated responsiveness is required if states are to mobilise societal backing and, consequently, policy continuity over time.

This duality poses a challenge to the social sciences which have tended to emphasise on one of the two dimensions. Profound insight into societal autonomy from, and unity of action displayed by states is deducible only by means of analysis departing from the domestic level. The huge varieties in state resources are thus primarily a function of state-society relations. Following this the coming sections will first look at how the state-society dichotomy has been perceived in the social sciences. Similar treatment is then given to inter-state relations. Both sub-sections will be concluded by pointing to the significance increasingly accorded to ideas and on the basis of this demonstrate the need for an institutional approach.

## 2.2 State and Society: Ideas as Institutional Intermediaries

Anglo-Saxon and continental European social science have generally treated the phenomenon of state rather differently. The former tends to equate state with government whereas the latter relates the concept with:

> the notion of the abstract, impersonal state as an entity or personality above and distinct from both government and governed; as an institution which is autonomous, formally co-ordinated and differentiated from other organisations which operate in a defined territory; as an object of universal service and respect; as the source of a distinct public morality.[17]

The most tangible aspects of statehood are found in the apparatus of state. Generally continental and Anglo-Saxon oriented social scientists would agree that the apparatus of state at least encompass the central administration, courts of justice and the police. Differences resurface when continental scholars advance the view that these bodies possess a distinct character vis-à-vis organisations of the civil sphere.

An intermediate view argues that states – while once displaying distinctive institutional traits vis-à-vis society at large – have lost most or all of this past distinctiveness. Although still sole holder of the legitimate prerogative of coercion within national territory as pointed out by Max Weber, a number of other traits seem to have either vanished or considerably weakened. As observed by Philippe Schmitter it seems no longer cogent to talk of unity of action and sovereignty as hallmarks of statehood as incoherence and competition is observed between governmental departments even while the nations they serve are faced with growing interdependence.[18] Other characteristics such as the capacity to defend national territory, the expression of universal interests of the population, unique patterns of recruitment and organisation and the association with a particular nation have never had much historical credence.

Other traits singled out as distinctive of statehood, however, still hold validity. States thus confer to their central institutions the power to act for the state in international affairs. Venues such as Intergovernmental Conferences (IGCs) are still largely reserved for Ministries of States and Foreign Affairs.

When dismissing the element of unity of action from our understanding of state, we move towards a pragmatic sectorised image which encompasses the executive, legislative and juridical branches of government and the collection of professional – largely government funded – organisations entrusted with the preparation, formulation, adoption and implementation of public policies.

In operational terms the state is thus reduced to a source of funding and politics is regarded as essentially being an exercise of either public distribution or public redistribution. This image corresponds perfectly with the mainstream definition of politics in the sixties which asserted that: 'politics is about the authoritative allocation of goods with binding effect upon society'. The centrality of the state in all political calculations, which has been another pluralist 'mantra', is retained since politics is seen as one of the two allocation mechanisms in a societal dichotomy allowing only for a market and a state sphere.

In emphasising the fragmentation and compartmentalisation of the state and political life at large, the monolithic perception of state is replaced by a demystifying image of a collection of public agencies constrained by political attempts of coordination by the executive, interacting with policy communities of affected interests often forging alliances against other state agencies.

This understanding of political 'practice' neglects what may be termed the cohesive dimension of politics which highlights institutions and structures holding the fabrics of society together by political means. Consensus formation, long-term agenda formation and even strategic development can thus hardly be accommodated within the standard behavioural understanding of politics and consequently the state.

As indicated above, the idea of the state is amorphous. Essentially the values embodied in respectively the continental and the Anglo-Saxon perception of state is connected to how the basic properties of society at large are regarded. As it shall be discussed below, a distinction can be drawn between notions based on either the concepts of community or association.

### 2.2.1 Society: Community versus Association

The concepts of community and association are vital when assessing the significance of state-society relations with regards to regional integration. If the electorate and the central actors behave only in accordance to selfish motives as suggested by pluralists, regional integration appears to be a relatively simple task. If, however, other factors like kinship, deep-rooted values resting on nationally founded 'characters' prevail over rational calculation at the different levels of the political system, regional integration by means of centrally initiated policies becomes highly complicated.

The regional integrative efforts of Western Europe following the signing of the treaties in the fifties, is commonly and officially regarded as a community of nation states seeking to evolve into 'an ever closer union'. Pioneer of regional integration studies, Karl W. Deutsch, defined integration as:

> The attainment, within a territory, of a 'sense of Community' and of institutions and practices strong enough and widespread enough to assure, for a 'long' time, dependable expectations of 'peaceful change' among its population.[19]

Communities, according to Deutsch, are bonded by a shared feeling of unity among the individual members of the group. Proponents of this vision of community are typically the sociological functionalist school as represented by Talcott Parsons and Robert K. Merton. Deutsch saw the making of 'community' as the key challenge posed to European and, for that matter, North Atlantic integration.

As opposed to community, the notion of association presumes no natural uniting factors. What has brought about association is rather the rational calculation of individuals recognising the mutual benefits of relaxing unconditional freedom endured on any man at the time of birth in exchange for some self-restraint backed up by potential societal sanctions. German sociologist Ferdinand Tönnies explores the distinction of the German equivalents as he notes:

> In Gemeinschaft they (the individuals) remain essentially united in spite of all separating factors, whereas in Geselschaft they are essentially separated in spite of all uniting factors.[20]

A Gemeinschaft perspective suggests that the state comes out of society whereas the Geselschaft angle would be inclined to regard the state as something which imposes itself on society. As a political ideal the nation state presupposes the abstract state image coupled with a national community. Although elite political cultures may either reflect a predominantly Gemeinschaft or Geselschaft understanding of groups and individuals, the case for broader national cultures has been discredited.[21]

While the notion of nation states may essentially be considered a political construct employed in the rhetoric of nationalism rather than an analytical category, state-society relations do diverge qualitatively between countries.

Economic historians have had some success in employing the intermediate category of 'institution' as an explanatory source of recurrence in the behaviour of market agents in distinct geographical settings. Institutions are thus seen as performing a role in economic transactions comparable to the role supposedly performed by the much more controversial and ambiguous notion of political culture in politics. Institutions are historically rooted and culturally embedded. Institutions can be altered but the direction of the alteration cannot be fully determined in advance and generally institutional properties exhibit a vast element of rigidity.

### 2.2.2 *Institutions as Societal Fabrics*
Conceptually the notion of 'institution' is addressed at two levels in both political science and economics. At one level institutions are

considered as either policy or market actors and sometimes even policy and market arenas. Another understanding of institutions concerns how actors *think* politics and economics. Economics has historically offered the most explicit application of institutional analysis. Since the methodological struggle at the turn of the century the concept of institution has been disputed but rarely ignored.

Thorstein Veblens's classic definition of institutions as 'habits of thought' is attractive in that it enables conceptual linkages to sociological theory on socialisation and discourse formation. The comprehensive nature of the above-mentioned definition, however, makes it somewhat difficult to operationalise because a wide range of phenomena may be designated as institutions. A methodology is thus needed to enable a distinction to be made between various forms of institutions.

Carl Menger distinguished between organic and pragmatic institutions where the former denotes 'habits of thought' or organisational frameworks which have emerged spontaneously as an unintended outcome by the actions of individuals and the latter refers to 'designed' institutions.[22] In addition he observed that institutions can either take on the character of an organisation, identified by operating through authority and control, or a habit, a routine or a social rule. Institutions may perform both a confining and enabling function in relation to the behavioural patterns of individuals.

Designed institutions with the character of an organisation cannot be adequately understood without explicit reference to the organic and non-organisational elements. The organic and non-organisational elements are in turn partly shaped by the designed and organisational frameworks. Any institutional analysis thus needs to be a dynamic analysis.

Pragmatic and organisational institutions are embedded in organic and non-organisational institutions. Organic and non-organisational institutions bear much resemblance to what David Soskice has designated 'Institutional Infrastructures'. He emphasises the level of trust and the duration of relationships between actors as the decisive variables when distinguishing between various national types of labour market systems.[23]

The methodology of Soskice makes implicit use of what is labelled the 'policy network approach' by the political science literature. The policy network approach aims at depicting the social functioning, development and interrelation of sectorally confined venues of elite interaction. It originates in works by Stein Rokkan from the sixties and more prominently in an article by Hugh Heclo from 1977. Its sociological underpinnings go back much further and boast prominent proponents such as Simmel and Levy-Strauss.[24]

Policy networks are simultaneously subject to institutional constraints in their mode of operation and constitute the venues where institutions are shaped in an essentially social process involving actors from contending elite segments.

In understanding pragmatic (designed) and organic institutions, knowledge about patterns of basic value-systems and frames of identification is essential. Institutional analysis thus requires social analysis! A social analysis in turn must offer a methodology for depicting the dynamics of value formation and change. Discourse analysis and the social construction approach pertain to explain how 'truth', 'science' and 'rationality' are socially constructed as discourses in power struggles between a wide range of actors and become institutionalised – for example, 'habits of thought' – reflected in social practice.

### 2.2.3   Ideas and Institutions

Institutionalisation of ideas as organic non-organisational 'habits of thought' is, according to Judith Goldstein and Robert O. Keohane possible at three levels: world views, principled beliefs and causal beliefs with the two latter often linked to the former.[25] World views consists of both normative, cosmological, ontological and ethical notions informing the identities of individuals. The great religions and scientific rationality are examples of world views. World views are sufficiently broad to accommodate opposing principled and causal beliefs. Christianity thus managed both to endorse and oppose slavery and the positivist paradigm has no problems containing contradicting Keynesian and monetarist causal assumptions about money supply, inflation and employment. World views exhibit a higher level of rigidity than more operational discourses such as principled beliefs and causal beliefs when it comes to fundamental alterations. This may in part be explained by the flexibility of world views in accommodating contending principled and causal beliefs as stated above. But world views in addition impinge so deeply on human identity that changes are hampered by perceptual, conceptual and other cognitive barriers thus making the introduction of new world views a time consuming and often bloody exercise.

The emphasis on ideas and institutions cannot deny material interests a huge importance both in domestic and international politics.

Interests require perception and identification, which is essentially a social process. Westerners are thus often stunned when they hear Muslim women speak of the respect – and implicitly gender equality – they enjoy in societies which with European eyes seem boldly repressive. While women would seem to have a natural interest in controlling the plight of their own lives and bodies no perception of such an interest seems to take hold in the majority of women in the Arab world. Marxists faced a similar problem as they failed to account for cooperative strategies pursued by labour movements in a number of capitalist countries following the Second World War. False class consciousness became their mechanic explanations given for the constantly postponed 'inevitable' revolution.

Institutions may curtail potential interests from actors. In the case of Islam a world belief institutionalised in marriage rituals, family patterns and civil law contravene female emancipation from becoming a focal point around which Arab women rally. But this interpretation reveals the Western outlook of this observer. One could thus equally claim that institutions are conducive in identifying the interests of actors. The general principle of individual sovereignty as reflected in the liberal human rights of the French revolution may consequently be said to constitute the philosophical (discursive) groundwork which had female emancipation as its nearly inevitable albeit unintended consequence.

The traditional image of interests as driving forces in social activity usually features the self-maximising individual. Running the fear of reinstating the widely discredited ideas of Maslow, it seems reasonable to suggest that individuals have some basic and absolute hierarchies with respect to personal interests. Although Maslow's 'need hierarchy' is highly biased towards western norms and values, his observations on subsistence nonetheless have some validity.[26] Food, shelter and perhaps even spouses must be considered needs which, disregarding all constraining and facilitating institutions, must be reckoned to materialise as articulated interests provided their provision are in short supply vis-à-vis levels required for subsistence.

Beyond these basic needs interests are socially constructed and based on institutionally embedded rationales such as 'profits', 'rationality' and group identification. States pursue perceived interests in international relations. Perceived interests are moulded by ideas, be they world views, principled beliefs or causal beliefs. Once institutionalised, however, perceived interests form stable reference points around which political activity is structured.

Discourse analysis and the social construction approach have their roots in the hermeneutic paradigm and consequently pose a challenge to the positivist (and behaviouralist) paradigm which emphasises rationality. An often advanced criticism of social constructivism point to the dangers of nihilism. The lack of 'social fixpoints' indicated by the nihilist metaphor, may partly be surmounted by stressing the rigidity of institutions. Institutions are thus the fixpoints of history and social analysis.

Institutions provide the key for a political economy understanding of the state which lies between the traditional abstract continental and the reductionist but operational Anglo-Saxon perception. States may thus by confined to a collection of designed and undesigned institutions characterised by internal fragmentation while simultaneously embedded in the social institutions of society at large resulting in some consistency across and in between the fundamental value systems of the elite and the electorate. What distinguishes the institutions of the state from the institutions of society at large is the socially constructed joint sense of purpose which – as will be discussed later – is subject to divergent interpretations and constant political attempts of reformulation.

## 2.3   State Rivalry: Ideas and Interests

Statehood is two dimensional. Besides domestic society states face other states. States are designated a key role in all theories of international relations. The main paradigms of international relations, 'realism' and 'interdependence', assign the state different degrees of dominance but nonetheless both recognise its pivotal role on all levels of analysis.

### 2.3.1   Realism and Ideas: The English School
While realism is widely associated to the concept of national interest, innovative proponents of the paradigm have tampered with the notion of ideas as a factor structuring power relations between states. The so-called 'English School of international relations' as represented by Hedley Bull, Maurice Wright and Reginald Vincent distinguishes three contending philosophical currents each representing different principled and causal beliefs on the relationship between states.[27] The three currents reflect the positions of Thomas Hobbs, Emmanuel Kant and Hugo Grotius respectively. The Hobbsian perspective is very much in line with traditional realist analysis whereas the Kantian

perspective makes a plea for the inclusion of the international community in regulating the affairs of man. Man is, according to the Kantian stance, created in the image of God and consequently shares a series of fundamentals such as commitment to a common morality and faith. Grotius likewise argues for a world order beyond the anarchy of Hobbs. While Grotius recognises the absence of world government he too, nonetheless, points to a common source of morality which may be employed as the constituent base for a system of international law safeguarding the interests of states.

The treaties of Osnabrück and Münster which constitute the Peace of Westphalia (1648) allegedly instituted a world order stressing sovereignty in line with the Hobbsian tradition and the principle of international law compatible with the followers of Grotius. In the wake of the Napoleonic Wars and the Congress of Vienna, international law was boosted even further perhaps at the expense of the autonomous state as portrayed by the Hobbsian camp. With the end of the Cold War and subsequent incidents of humanitarian intervention as witnessed in Iraq, Somalia and Bosnia, we may finally be entering a stage in international relations where the Kantian perspective is gaining prominence.[28]

For our purpose the theoretical significance of this perspective is the appreciation that ideas matter in the basic operations of the international system. Any change from one philosophical current to another in the ideals of international relations as held by key players, is thus bound to affect the character of, and distribution of power resources among, actors. States excelling under 'Hobbsian' conditions, for example, will have to nurture a whole new set of policy instruments in order to get by under 'Kantian' conditions.

### 2.3.2 Interdependence and Ideas: Post-Hegemonic Regime Theory

Opposing the realist paradigm a school stressing the interdependence of both states and other actors gained ground in the sixties and seventies. Transnationalism is the interdependent approach to the study of regional integration. Its proponents have concentrated mainly on specific forms of international (transnational) cooperation. This is illustrated particularly well by the application of the approach within the field of regime theory as discussed below.[29]

Advocates of transnationalism reject the notion of national interest. Instead they turn to national political systems and identify which political actors participate in the decision making of different policy areas, and how they affect the EU policy outcomes. States are considered important actors on the international arena albeit not the only ones. Other actors include multinational corporations, international organisations, 'transgovernmental bureaucratic alliances', transnational pressure groups and even national interest groups. In addition states are viewed as being fragmented rather than monolithic and as such conform to the pluralist view of domestic politics.

Interest fragmentation appears to be the common denominator between the interdependence approach and pluralism. At the onset this also appears to be the case in the stated institutional continuation of the interdependence approach: regime theory. Regime theory seeks to explain the growth of international institutions in relation mainly to economic issues such as trade, money, labour and energy. As in the state-society discussion institutions denote here both organic and pragmatic forms. The GATT (WTO) and the World Bank derive their institutional properties both out of the fact that there is a codified system of rules administered by the respective secretariats in Geneva and Washington and a broad acceptance of these rules and procedures which enables the organisations to expand in both scope and membership. This has been achieved in spite of the fact that the secretariat exhibits virtually no effective sanctional remedies and certain key states have consistently performed poorly in international trade throughout the last two decades. While some states experience that international trade is increasingly becoming a hot item on national policy agendas, withdrawal or similar opportunist behaviour has still not occurred. The observation that international hegemons – purely out of self-interest – sponsor international 'sectoral' regimes is fully compatible with pluralist orthodoxy. Robert Keohane's study of 1985, however, suggests regimes continue to perform after the decline of the sponsoring hegemon.[30] While the formation of international regimes in Keohane's book follows the usual *interest → power → regime* formula, the ability of these to provide normative frameworks constraining the behaviour of states indicates an autonomous role for ideas and institutions in international relations which cannot simply be reduced to institutional rigidity. Theoretical convergence can thus be observed between branches of both realism and interdependence in their appreciation of ideas and institutions. As this conveniently happens to be the conclusion on the examination of writings on state–societal relations I will now attempt to construct an institutional conceptual framework which is able to contain the duality of statehood while allowing for both an actor and a structural dimension.

## 2.4  Towards an Institutional Understanding of the State

States interact on the international arena and in addition they seem to display some societal autonomy and unity of action. Deliberate co-ordination efforts account for some of the apparent unity but may not, on the other hand, be conducive for societal autonomy! Profound insight on the societal autonomy and unity of action displayed by states is deducible only by means of analysis departing from the domestic level as no theory of international relations has managed to take into account the huge variety in state resources. The international system nonetheless provides the basis of much state legitimacy which is transformed into the domestic setting often with considerable impacts as witnessed in relation to project 1992 and the EMU.

A political economy approach to regional integration needs to explicitly appreciate what has been termed 'the double anchorage of the state' in order to grasp the societal complexity simultaneously constraining and encouraging regional integration.[31] But how may we accommodate unity of action by means of societal cohesion with the domestic reality of actor plurality and state fragmentation?

### 2.4.1  A Theory of the State: The Domestic Arena

Modern state theory – which is strikingly cautious in employing the state concept – has sought to handle the paradoxical appearance of both coherence and incoherence in state action at the domestic level. Modern state theory has its origins in the Neomarxist debates of the seventies featuring on the one hand Nico Poulantzas and Louis Althusser and on the other hand Ralph Milibrand. While Poulantzas and Althusser were structural in their appreciation of state-society relations Ralph Milibrand advocated a somewhat more institutional outlook compatible, perhaps, with neopluralist network theory.[32]

A parallel observation can be made with regard to the respective positions of Ernesto Laclau and Chantal Mouffe[33] and James March and Johan P. Olsen.[34] The former thus stress the formation of hegemonic projects which structure the articulation of policies across policy sectors by providing 'fix-points of meaning'. This ensures a high degree of unity in the action of formally disparate layers of government in capitalist societies.

In *Re-discovering Institutions* March and Olsen depict an image of politics stressing its essential social nature. They nonetheless maintain a vital aspect of the pluralist legacy in denouncing the element of structure as suggested by the notion of hegemonic projects. Institutions thus interpret their own rationale in a process which is simultaneously constrained and facilitated by existing rationale, the institutional environment and broader categories of societal norms and values. The endogenous dynamic of this process stresses the fundamental character of polities as fragmented both across and within traditional policy sectors. The issue of aggregation is not explicitly approached in a comprehensive manner, but just as government agencies are tied together by a unified, hierarchically ordered command and control structure, policy sectors seem to rely on mechanisms of informal organisation with power resource distributed unevenly among participants as demonstrated by the policy network literature. Organic entities interrelated by means of policy networks thus ensure an ordered institutional environment which provides frameworks for 'meaning-coordination' and compatibility.

Articulating 'ideology' and interpreting 'purpose' are, according to Laclau and Mouffe and March and Olsen respectively, the essence of 'institutional' dynamics.[35] An articulation strategy is by character outbound. Articulating 'institutions' strive for hegemony while the interpretation perspective suggests an inward orientation as 'institutions' attempt to establish coherence by discursive remedies. The extended organisational culture perspective offered by March and Olsen focuses on the design process which is a social, albeit not entirely, chaotic process. The interpretation perspective, however, goes beyond mere endogenous organisational processes. The institutional environment thus plays a pivotal role when organisations position themselves. In addition the 'purpose' which is considered 'valid' by one organisation will inform its behaviour vis-à-vis other organisations.

Interpreting institutions use articulating institutions as waypoints in their purpose definition process. Formal hierarchy among institutions dictates who may potentially assume the role of 'ideology' articulators. Some institutions are prohibited from access to the agenda formation arena. This would be the case of implementing branches of national central bureaucracies. Programme implementing bodies would thus usually refrain from pitting their skills against central departments on broad policy issues. Informal hierarchy similarly defines institutions as either participants or bystanders in the broad political economic policy spectacles. This would be the case for most service producing ministries. Consequently Ministries of Health rarely engage in struggles over ideological hegemony vis-à-vis

Ministries of Finance.

Institutions holding keys for vital components in the regulation of the economy have privileged status as potential articulators. Institutional political economy identifies the state, the labour market and the financial system at large as the access points to the arena where struggles on the overall design of the political economy occurs. The product market in addition embodies institutionalised practices stemming from the character of the goods subject to exchange. These institutionalised practices in turn define ideals on the design of both strictly market and non-market institutions. These ideals eventually constitute a base for political action congregating actors aggregating a loose but joint sense of purpose, articulating policy discourses within the framework of what may be termed a rationale eventually informing the behaviour of agents.

All industrial political economies contain both a state, a labour market, a product market and a financial system. In addition these political economic focal points are interconnected with, in particular, the state as an ever adjacent factor. The four pillars of political economies may be regarded as spheres which simultaneously interact, co-exist and compete for societal hegemony. Key participants in the financial systems sphere, for example, thus aspire to subdue labour market interests vis-à-vis 'money' interests.[36] At the same time 'money' and 'labour' are highly interdependent and have a broad range of mutual interests (macroeconomic stability, governability and high growth rates).

Complete hegemony is never achieved in advanced political economies, however, one sphere is likely to achieve relative supremacy over the others. Relative supremacy does not imply that remaining spheres are marginalised in national political economies. Rather relative supremacy denotes the position when the institutions of one sphere have managed to articulate a socio-economic frame of meaning which enjoys broad acceptance and as such constitutes the beacon from which interpreting institutions take bearing. The remaining potentially articulating spheres simultaneously challenge and adapt to (interpret) the dominant socio-economic discourse articulated.

Discourse articulation is essentially an exercise of power. Contending spheres are accordingly engaged in power struggles. Power struggles may be fought out in pragmatic institutions by discursive remedies and their settlement may be a product of overall structural conditions. But power struggles always involve actors.

Beyond 'spheres' and 'institutions' lie actors be they individuals or organisations. Discourses originate from actors constrained or conduced by institutionalised 'habits of thought' and previous 'practices' (perceived history). Structures determine how actors, institutionalised 'habits of thought' and previous 'practices' relate to one another. Actors of the sphere of the financial system include central banks, private, public and savings banks, insurance companies and the associated regulatory agencies. These actors are in turn naturally connected to the corporate sector exposed to international competition. Their mode of interaction is partly given by the character of the subject of exchange. The money spheres exchange money. This gives rise to a set of institutionalised assumptions and ideals about social management – governance – and power (how and why is discussed in section 3). Spheres foster rationales which are key structural components of advanced political economies. Rationales thus link spheres and actors with institutions.

Rationales are to be regarded as 'meta-discourses' which frame a number of contending discourses on governance strategy. They originate in spheres and constitute important structural components of Western political economies. Institutional features of one sphere may spill over to other spheres as rationales compete and attempt to colonise one another. Within the labour sphere at the European level three governance strategies are identified in this study (see chapters 3 and 4 on social protection and social dialogue). In the first strategy the functional group strives to seize influence on the affairs of the state in order to manipulate the market. In the second strategy the social partners and the state engage in a process of coordinate governance. And finally in the last strategy the functional group engages in deliberate attempts to articulate a labour based socio-economic discourse. Each of these strategies correspond to a particular rationale (this is discussed thoroughly in chapter 5).

Political economies are dynamic systems. Relative supremacy is subject to alteration over time both with regard to degree and holder. In terms of degree the dominant rationale may either operate under conditions of relative tranquillity or be subject to severe charges from contending rationales. When facing serious challenges from one of the other rationales, institutions of the dominant rationale are subject to constraints as their impact on interpreting institutions is less pervasive than under conditions of discoursive tranquillity. A prolonged period with repetitive challenges from contending rationales may eventually produce a shift in relative supremacy as one set of institutions may be ousted as chief articulators and replaced by institutions of another rationale. The stability – or configurational volatility – of political economies over time is intrinsically linked to state-society relations and the overall question of state coherence.

### 2.4.2   A Theory of the State: The International Arena

Some degree of state coherence is achieved in an interplay between articulating and interpreting institutions. The capacity for achieving coherence by either discursive or coercive means depends on state structure and the societal integration of the state.

Table 1 displays a typology for coherence in state action. Two variables are listed: 'societal integration' and 'state structure'. 'State structure' in this context denotes the formal status of various agencies and their interrelation. The most salient element of state structure is the overall organising principle of central-local relations. States thus usually conform to either the federate, confederate or unitary ideal. Within these overarching structuring principles great variances occur.

*Table 1*

| Unity of action? | | State structure | |
|---|---|---|---|
| | | *Centralised* | *Decentralised* |
| *Societal* | High | Diachronic coherence Synchronic coherence | Diachronic coherence Synchronic incoherence |
| *Integration* | Low | Diachronic incoherence Synchronic coherence | Diachronic incoherence Synchronic incoherence |

Unitary states may thus rely on well defined vertical chains of authority and control employed as a counter-device for sectoral fragmentation. Alternatively unitary states may employ governance mechanisms utilising socially embedded consensus formation capacities and thus adopt a less stringent system of vertical authority and control. State structure is thus a complex measurement of the organisational rationale of state apparatuses which goes beyond formal structure. The Danish unitary state may thus be grouped as 'decentral' due to the vast de facto autonomy of local government and the modest impact of formal hierarchy between individual Ministries when acting in international settings.

The 'societal integration' variable follows up on the classical 'society-state' dichotomy subject for dispute at the height of the controversy between traditional Marxists and proponents of the neocorporatist approach in the seventies and eighties. As stated in the discussion of the nation state, political culture is a key pointer for consistency between popular values – associated with civil society – and elite values. The industrial culture identified by Dyson performs a similar task with respect to the managerial elite associated with the market.[37]

In operational terms correspondence between the social base and the key articulating institutions within a given sphere is the essence of societal integration. 'Stray' institutions articulating frameworks of meaning bypassing or inconsistent with the associated power agency will sooner or later find themselves at odds with their social base. The perverted version of the state rationale as operating in France thus exhibits a weak legislature and a strong executive as the *petite bourgeoisie* has failed to provide consistent backing. Societal integration ultimately determines the capacity for achieving coherence by discursive means.

Each of the four cells in Table 1 contain a unique mix of two types of coherence. Diachronic coherence/incoherence relate to the stability in the pursuit of national policy objectives (national interest) over time. Synchronic coherence/incoherence refer to the extent to which actors – emanating from the same state – act in accord at a given point in time.

A highly centralised state structure is likely to be a response to, or product of, modest societal integration. Similarly a decentralised state structure may be a prerequisite for a high level of societal integration as reciprocity is the foundation for political legitimacy (with regard to regional autonomy, autonomy of organised societal groupings, citizens rights, minorities etc.). States consequently cannot be expected to adhere to the four cells randomly. Most West European states will fit the categories combining either 'low societal integration' and 'centralised state structure' or 'high societal integration' and 'decentralised state structure'. Russia on the other hand may be said to fit the category 'low societal integration' and 'decentralised state structure' while Singapore is a rare case of 'high societal integration' and 'centralised state structure'.

While international relations can serve to amplify national coherence, they may also contribute to a disruption in national discursive equilibrium. Articulating agencies thus use international relations in their quest for relative supremacy.[38] The deregulation of international financial transactions initiated in the wake of the first oil crisis produced different responses in individual states. While virtually all OECD countries relaxed foreign exchange control the impact on national financial regimes varied due to the differences in institutional mixes already in operation. It is thus difficult to maintain a functional explanation for the globalisation of finance since effects have been very different for individual countries. The spread of financial deregulation must consequently be regarded as the spread of an idea which was received by proponents of particular governance rationales and employed in national power struggles.[39] The breakdown of Bretton Woods resulted in the erection of regional arrangements such as ERM. This altered the position of the money market rationale vis-à-vis the labour market rationale in a number of European countries as they had to take on sponsorship of an exchange-rate regime which had previously been upheld by the USA.

The internal market scheme may conversely have altered the position between the money rationale and the product market rationale with the growing emphasis on 'transparent competition' supported by public 'umpire-ship'. The public procurement and the standardisation elements of the internal market scheme combined with the establishment of a regulatory hierarchy instituted by the 'Cassis de Dijon' ruling of the European Court of Justice, signals a governance rationale featuring market transparency and a minimisation of transaction cost.

To sum up, national political economies exhibit particular configurations of rationales. France has traditionally displayed a strong state power rationale while Germany is characterised by a constitutionally underpinned money market rationale which at times has been supplemented by a labour market rationale. Regional integration inevitably upsets the national political-economic equilibrium. An exposure of the product market will thus ramify into the labour and money markets. At the same time configurational convergence is a precondition for major integrative progress. The pace and direction of regional integrative schemes is thus a product of the ongoing struggle between contending rationales which may expand their respective constituencies from a national to a regional base. Emphasis must accordingly be on how policies are informed by various rationales and how contending rationales attempt to colonise individual policies. Political struggles are not fought out in a vacuum. States are central participants particularly when national frontiers are transgressed as in the case of the EU. States display different institutional qualities which is a function of state-society relations severely affecting their capacity for action – in both the domestic and the international realm.

## 3   MARKETS: MICRO FOUNDATIONS AND MACRO INTERDEPENDENCE

Markets may be understood either as an abstract notion of exchange-relations or geographically confined venues of commodity specific transactions. As previously stated advanced economic systems are comprised of at least three distinct broad market categories out of which two cannot be characterised as handlers of commodities.

Markets are national. Exchanges take place between agents from different national markets, but dispute settlement concerning key institutional mechanisms such as terms of exchange, property rights and liability, are usually conferred to a national arena – often identified in the sales contract. National markets are interconnected and consequently interdependent. The degree of interdependence is a function of national strategies for respectively the exposure and sheltering of particular domestic markets.

European labour markets are traditionally directly sheltered in the sense that alien workers face restrictions when attempting to enter a foreign labour market. Indirectly public procurement, tariff and non-tariff barriers to trade and industry subsidies have acted as potent instruments of national labour market protection. These barriers, however, seem set to crumble in the wake of the Single European Market (SEM) and successive GATT/WTO rounds of global trade liberalisation. Informally, language, culture and lifestyle differences have in addition served to keep labour markets distinctly national.

Europe's financial markets have, until recently, displayed some variance with regard to their degree of openness. British banking has traditionally been oriented towards world markets while German banking has considered it more prudent to cater for the needs of German industry. Markets for money are more diverse than markets for labour. Some segments of national money markets are thus highly interdependent in all EU member states. This is the case of foreign exchange and lending rates. A key segment of financial systems, however, seems to remain national, that is, the allocation of capital to commercial operations and the closely associated market for firms.[40]

Product markets are driving the globalisation of the economy. As a rule, product markets are highly exposed to foreign competition in the OECD although sheltering occurs within areas such as agriculture, construction and defence contracting. Structural changes in Western economies have chiefly been identified in relation to the operation of products markets where new technologies and management techniques have reportedly mandated a change in the mode of production from fordism to post-fordism. Inter-firm relations and craft-centred production methods have allegedly spurred as new technology has enabled a shift in the cost-efficiency of small scale production.[41] While obstacles to the free movement of goods have diminished, markets for final goods and capital goods are subject to different trajectories as the former are easily adopted to local preferences while capital goods/semi-manufacturers may be customised to specific user requirements in a mutual learning process enabled by intimate user-producer links.[42] These linkages may be crucial for the innovative capacity of national product markets and thus constitute an informal sheltering mechanism vis-à-vis foreign market entrants.

**3.1 The Micro Foundation of Markets**

Markets, as we know them, rest on general institutions stipulating regimes for property rights, transactions and liability. Economic institutions are founded on social norms.[43] Social norms are culturally embedded. Jon Elster argues that 'Social norms offer considerable scope for skill, choice, interpretation and manipulation.' While individual action is informed and even constrained by social norms a mechanistic understanding of their behavioural impact is widely rejected. Social norms are simultaneously informing and adapted by collective action. Market relations and conduct of societal governance comprise complex patterns of individual and collective action. In the previous sections I introduced the notion of rationales as 'meta-discourses which frame contending ideals on governance strategy.' In this section I will strive to add some flesh to the 'rationale' metaphor. In the following each of the three markets will be examined more closely.

*3.1.1 Labour Markets*
Labour markets are subject to politically instigated regulation. However, labour markets simultaneously operate as a private contractual arrangement as agreed either individually or collectively between employers and employees. Yet states have a significant saying in the conclusion of particularly collective agreements while employer and employee representatives have significant roles in the making of the legal provisions providing the overall guidelines for labour market affairs.

Following the First World War, participation of the employer and employee organisations in the formal institutions of the state grew significantly. Labour market organisations were invited to participate in the drawing up of legislation particularly in the aftermath of the Second World War. A pattern prevails suggesting that consecutive conclusions of agreements without severe social unrest provided the ticket to state acceptance – thus state recognition followed a period of partial labour market self-regulation.[44]

An ongoing dialogue between state and labour market organisations has emerged. In some countries this evolved into frameworks for concerted action. Concerted action denotes institutionalised bargaining between labour market organisations and state. It usually implies that labour moderates its short term demands vis-à-vis employers in exchange for long-run state concessions with regard to future access to, and participation in, general economic policy making.[45] Concerted action constitutes the most elaborate tripartite labour market regime found in advanced political economies. Ideological preference and institutional short-comings has led most OECD countries to opt for less 'extensive' approaches. Concerted action is a product of historical contextual factors. Hence this type of arrangement was apparently considered more as an ideal in pioneer states during the seventies than today.

There is a relationship between the configuration of the industrial relations system and the structure and functioning of labour markets and consequently the costs induced upon companies when responding to structural change.[46] Measured on variables like recruitment patterns, the possibility of reallocating labour, the flexibility of the shopfloor, the qualification process and finally dismissals and labour turnover, the structure and functioning of labour markets on the enterprise level seem to depend on:

- job control: who has it and at what level does it operate
- the structure of qualifications and jobs within the company
- organisational mode of labour
- the pattern of interest representation
- conflict regulation and the degree of formal regulation within industrial relations.[47]

Labour markets thus constitute a distinct sub-system in advanced economies with specific features regarding agent characteristics, modes of interaction and general pragmatic institutions on property rights, transactions and liability. In spite of cross-national institutional divergence common fundamental qualities characterise labour markets throughout the EU. First and foremost market mechanisms do not determine wage levels. Necessary impurities permeate this market as it would otherwise self-destruct as pointed out by Karl Polanyi and Geoffrey Hodgson. Labour markets trade time and skills of people. Individual preferences and trade-offs on time consumption and skill acquisition is a function of social processes. Beyond struggles for subsistence – which is rarely encountered in advanced economies – individual preferences are primarily shaped by leisure, family and lifestyle values rather than market dictates. In sum the skill and time consumption trade-off of labourers, which constitute the 'commodities' of labour markets, are shaped by social rather than market pressures.

In order to avoid constant disequilibrium labour markets are organised by the state and the social partners in cartel-like arrangements interacting on the basis of political rather than market power. Social organisation is the vehicle for political power. The logic of interaction ideally involves representatives from the two sides of industry with the state acting as mediator. Representatives from employers and employees rely on opponents having a fair grip of their constituency if negotiations are to be fruitful. Unlike genuine network arrangements industrial relations aim at preserving clear lines of demarcation between participants in order to uphold legitimacy vis-à-vis constituencies. Essentially this makes for relations of mutual dependencies while simultaneously stressing the importance of maintaining a strong internal power base. Hence, the social partners rely on social force to engage in bargaining processes, the outcome of which is determined by political power resources.

### 3.1.2 Money Markets

As in the case of labour, money cannot be regarded or analysed as a commodity. Unlike labour, money is a symbol of value. Economists argue that ideally the value of money is a reflection of wealth produced by labour.[48] Markets for money are regulated at several levels. First and foremost, central banks issue money and defend their nominal value. This is done by measures designed to retain public confidence in the monetary system ranging from the production of notes and coins, in a manner preventing attempts of counterfeiting to joint intervention on money markets with governments aiming at restoring disrupted equilibrium on the LM curve.

Similar interventionist instruments are employed at currency markets, often reinforced by international collaborative arrangements such as the now defunct Bretton Woods and the ERM.

Secondly, money markets are regulated at the level of the commercial banking sector. Banks are key players on the money market but subject to – rather than co-operator of – the umpire function performed by central banks. Commercial banks are entrusted with the task of running the monetary circuits of advanced economies. The daily operations of these circuits are vital for the maintenance of the stabilising functions in relation to the LM curve. Consequently the banking sector is subject to vigorous regulation by the state and sometimes even semi-autonomous industry bodies.

The third level of regulation concerns the capital allocation functions of financial systems. Financial institutions are key holders of both listed and unlisted stocks and in addition channel both long and short term credits to firms. With the advent of arrangements inspired by venture capital financial institutions increasingly find themselves as direct providers of equity finance to high risk firms.

National banking systems have been subject to an immense pressure due to the deregulation process and the prominence of the free capital movement discourse. The effects of this on individual financial systems have varied as national institutional infrastructures have influenced the character of the adaptation process. German banking will consequently not completely resemble American or British banking as an outcome of integration even though the dominant discourse associated with the globalisation of banking is biased towards a British or American styled system.

John Zysman identifies three approaches to political-economic management in industrial countries: (1) A state-led path with developmental objectives in which the distribution of costs and gains is imposed by political manipulation of the market; (2) A negotiated path with a corporatist flavour in which there are explicit bargains amongst elites representing segments of society; and (3) a company-led approach with the government principally a regulator and umpire. Political settlements are largely left to the market, although the state often provides some compensation to uncomplaisant losers. The state-led path involves a capital allocation system relying on bank credits which are granted subject to quotas or interest rates established by governments. Such a system operated in France in the early eighties. The negotiated approach rests on a financial system with banks as key holders of industry equity shares. This fits with ample empirical evidence on German bank-industry relations. Finally, the market-led path presupposes a dynamic stock market serving the main capital allocation needs of industry – much in line with the British tradition.[49]

While these clear cut categories may not fit as neatly as in the early eighties when the study was conducted, evidence suggests that national systems follow distinct trajectories in the transformation process provoked by globalisation. In a study of European venture capital by Michael Kluth and Jørn Andersen (1997b) the image of national financial markets following national trajectories of adaptation when catering for new policy and/or market demands is supported. It is thus concluded that the operations of venture capital firms in the three case countries – France, Germany and the United Kingdom – reveal important differences regarding organisation, investment strategy and overall importance (demand). Global venture capital is far from homogeneous. Investment is still predominantly domestic in character. Only 13.5 per cent of the total funds managed by EVCA (European Venture Capital Association) members in 1990 was invested outside the venture capitalist's home countries. This is hardly surprising, as venture fund management requires certain skills and is ultimately a business learned by doing investments within certain industries – often confined to a limited geographical area.

Venture capital in Germany is thus used as a device to strengthen basic features of the political economy rather than changing it. The so-called 'Mittelstand' constituting German SMEs in manufacturing have traditionally been tied to the corporate sector through intimate supplier networks conducive for strong user-producer linkages. Yet many Mittelstand firms have had to operate in a fairly volatile business environment because users of their products may abandon them since they rarely enjoy mutual ownership links as in the case of the corporate sector. A large section of the Mittelstand have therefore conformed to, and constituted a base for, a pure market rationale. With the German flavour of venture capital high technology members of the Mittelstand will increasingly be subject to the intimacy of the bank-industry relations dictated by the money market rationale. Consequently this aspect of 'financial globalisation' serves to maintain the German ability to conduct 'Banking as usual'.

The British approach to introducing venture capital relies on market dynamics allowing for state intervention only in relation to perceived market failures. The dominant product market rationale thus responded favourably to the addition of a foreign institutional component originating in a largely compatible political economic setting – that is, the USA.

In France the state has clearly been the driving force in identifying the problems of capital allocation to innovative SMEs and consequently attempted to devise a solution through the instruments traditionally employed in national economic management. An investment insurance scheme – SOFARIS – has thus been created as a government agency which guarantees bank credits to firms. Once again the central planning institutions of the Republic, embedded in the offices and grand corps of finance and the première 'crowded out' the policy arena thus leaving all other potential actors passive in anticipation of central initiatives.[50]

Money markets are essentially subdued social factors such as trust and confidence. Information is the key variable in money market operations. To some extent this applies for all market operations but in money markets information assumes extraordinary importance as the utility of the traded 'commodity' – money – is a function of embedded confidence. What is traded is not printed paper, stamped metals or encrypted bits but accumulated confidence. The nature of money is thus social rather than that of a tangible artefact as in the case of goods.

Vendors of money in addition face severe informational problems rendering the financial sector impertinent for standard pricing techniques. The price of credit is thus not a function of the character of the 'commodity'. Similarly aggregate supply-demand determined pricing functions are largely useless in a sector where each business engagement is evaluated on its own merits. It is thus the overall operation and financial shape of the buyer that dictates the price.

Continuous information flows are intrinsic to money market dealings involving credits or capital allocation. Contracts typically extend over a long time and the seller – that is, the supplier of money – is in a position of having made his or her full commitment at the beginning of the engagement. Bankers and other providers of finance have an interest in controlling key parameters of the capital or credit recipients. This has found its most vivid expression in German finance-industry relations where the major banks exercise very active ownership of firms in which they have major stakes. The venture capital market system as developed particularly in California and the northeast of the USA reveals a similar pattern.

Users of credit and capital are often required to disclose information about their operations to suppliers. This poses a liability as capital and credit suppliers may serve competing firms. Users consequently choose their financial partners with care and would be inclined to prefer long-term relationships involving mutual trust and confidence, enhancing modes of interactions involving regular meetings in a manner resembling intimate networks.

### 3.1.3 Product Markets

Product markets comprise markets for capital, consumer and intermediate goods. Agents operating in product markets include manufacturers, distributors and retailers of goods. Product markets are harder to capture as reflecting a particular indigenous rationale because they are often colonised by contending rationales – hence it may be more appropriate to speak of a pure market rather than a product market rationale since the association between sphere and rationale is more ambiguous than in the case of the two factor markets discussed above.

Product markets appear residual due to their fragmentation. Following earlier attempts of delineating this category at least three sectors can be identified. These are agriculture, manufacturing and service activities such as retail and distribution.

Agriculture and manufactured goods are subject to quite different conditions. Agriculture in the OECD usually employs only limited amounts of labour as productivity has increased tremendously in the past century. Farms are often family businesses and the main production input is land which is a finite good. Agriculture is, in addition, subject to uncontrollable constraints such as weather conditions and the production cycle cannot be abrogated, thus making planning essential and rigidity considerable. A case could be made that farming is prone for submitting to the state power rationale with its emphasis on planning. The Common Agricultural Policy (CAP) lends support for such claims and the OECD-wide sheltering of farm products suggests that this sector prefers regularity for volatility. The extractive industries share some of the characteristics of agriculture in that minerals are depletable – analogous to the finite nature of land – and key variables are beyond the control of producers such as the location of production sites.

Retail and local distribution is not directly exposed to international competition. This applies to a number of manufacturers – and agricultural producers – as well. World market exposure and the overall state of competition affects a given sector with regard to preferences on transaction costs, market transparency and innovation.

Sheltered market segments may display oligopolistic patterns of operations and consequently be indifferent to high transaction costs as they can be fully recovered. High transaction costs may support particular social structures and thus serve the interests of certain social and/or political groupings. As market forces provide no impetus for changing such institutionalised rigidity, product markets may come to endure sustained operations under these conditions. Such product markets would be under the influence of a state power rationale.

Market transparency comprise, *ceteris paribus*, a greater advantage for new market entrants than existing players. Market intransparency has often been offered as explanation for the exceptionally strong position of Japanese manufacturers on their domestic market in spite of the fact that Japan complies to all GATT/WTO and OECD agreements on international trade. Intransparency may consequently be employed as a political or social tool by national manufacturers to block entry by foreign competitors.

Product markets displaying informal and formal hierarchies and networks between participants would, insofar as these are socially underpinned, be subject to a money market rationale. When politically nurtured and reinforced rather than socially embedded, product markets are subject to either a state power or a labour market rationale.

In sum, product markets constitute a somewhat residual category characterised by the emphasis on market transparency and low transaction costs, albeit governance rationales stemming from the state, labour and in particular money markets may have a severe effect on, for example, the duration and levels of trust in linkages between agents.

## 4   STATES, MARKETS AND GOVERNANCE

In our discussion on states the term 'rationale' was introduced. Rationales as 'meta-discourses' are associated to the three broad market categories outlined above and the state. Rationales constitute structuring devices in political economies exhibiting institutional contradiction, complexity and rigidity.

Given this complexity 'New Institutionalists' such as James March and Johan Olsen express amazement at the continuous functioning of societies as is the case in the Western World. They ascribe this to the workings of institutions.

In economic history and evolutionary institutional economics societal diversity is emphasised as a vital element ignored, for example, by mainstream economics. It is often argued that neoclassical economists are either misled or plain stupid when continuously proposing roughly similar policies to countries featuring very different institutional settings. An institutionalist response may stress that neoclassical economics constitutes a worldwide highly codified – and hence standardised – discourse.

Alternatively scientific discourse such as economics may be said to display certain basic properties of the 'material reality'. Laboratory life, as pointed out by Berger and Luckmann, is informed by codified assumptions about the behaviour of matter, that is basic causal views. New knowledge about matter generated by experiments will tend to reproduce causal views while still revealing new insight on the matter in question. Likewise the dominant paradigm in economics reflects and reproduces scientific discourse underpinned by political benefactors while at the same time revealing valid knowledge about 'societal reality'. Market is a broadly accepted metaphor for a particular type of exchange relation which is upheld as ideal and approximates real life transactions in a wide number of segments in contemporary Western societies. Core sectors of economic systems in Western societies would include labour markets, money markets and product markets. These markets – together with the state – comprise structural components each holding particular institutional properties. As structural components they are inevitable given contemporary modes of production, and consequently a source of societal convergence between countries of 'the Western World'. The structures identified by mainstream economics are here taken to be material realities.

Their institutional features, however, are socially constructed, hence subject to diversity and alteration although exhibiting considerable rigidity. Institutional attributes contained in rationales would as a minimum include ideals on governance and assumptions about agencies of power.

Following the discussion on labour markets it appears that the associated rationale in a pure form would stress power bargaining – in economic discourse comparable to oligopoly – as governance ideal with social force is the chief power agent. Money markets, with their dependence on trust, confidence and information exchange feature the network mode of governance as ideal. Networks often exhibit unevenly distributed power resources, hence controlling networks becomes the agency of power. Product markets advance the notion of the pure market as governance ideal and property rights – or owner-ship – the power agency. Finally, the state rationale resorts to classical hierarchy – a clear line of command and responsibility – and power agency is the embedded, principally equal, rights accorded in citizen-ship.

Principal market agents are bearers of particular rationales. The elites of unions and employer associations constitute the prime agents in oligopolistic labour markets. Without well-established bearers market rationales have little chance of making an impact on national political economic discourse. The USA, with its lack of organised labour power and highly fragmented employers, features no signifi-cant labour market rationale. Likewise most South American countries with their inadequate banking systems until recently could boast little in the way of national money market rationales. Purely agrarian societies are similarly deprived of product market rationales and civilian power entities like the European Union are unlikely to succumb to a strong state power rationale.

Bearers, or prime agents, may lend support from particular segments of the political economic systems. Using finance as an example, a money market rationale is first and foremost campaigned by central and major private banks. Benefactors are likely to be the internationally exposed corporate sector as stable exchange rates are conducive to foreign trade and sophisticated finance-industry rela-tions may work as a safeguard against hostile take-overs by foreign competitors. The corporate sector, represented by business associ-ations and key firms, would jointly with the political and administrative vanguard of the sector at the level of state, that is, the Ministry of Industry, consequently constitute the clients of the key actors campaigning the money market rationale.

Clients may be more or less explicit in their support for a given rationale. Approached from a traditional sociological perspective, clients apparently constitute distinct social bases with an associated institutional expression. In the case of the state power rationale the associated client actors is the traditional middle class typically includ-ing members of the professions while owners of small businesses and farmers adhering to the product market rationale advocate trans-parency in market relations, minimal regulation and respect for private property. The former's expression of power is either political parties competing for seats in parliament – which may pass on author-ity to the executive – or lobbying. The labour market rationale is based on labour (the working class) which seek to exercise power through the mobilisation of social forces. Finally the money market rationale derives its support from 'big' business where 'money talks'!

For the purpose of this study social base in itself is of minor importance as developments in the advanced political economies have served to delude traditional categories. Wage earners thus no longer struggle for survival at the level of subsistence as salaries have increased with the overall level of welfare. The traditional worker consequently hovers between a middle and a labour class identity.[51] Similarly, the separation of ownership from control in industry serves to debilitate the border between the middle class and the 'capitalist' class.[52]

Social base, strata and class are still valid as categories in sociological taxonomies but as political economic entities they mainly serve as historical points of reference which are employed in the social construction of meaning in a largely negative sense by proponents of various rationales. Political opponents are thus often designated as representatives of this or that class whereas contenders of particular rationales rarely apply the terminology on their own constituency!

Client bases derives their analytical importance from the fact that they each reflect a particular governance ideal based on perceived sources of power. The 'liberal' profession is in political terms associated with the classical democratic ideal subscribing to the 'one man one vote' principle. Individuals are ultimate holders of power accorded by *citizenship*. Labour is by contrast seen as politically reflecting the 'functional democracy' ideal according to which groups may attain the status of a *social force*. Social groups can, however, only realise their power potential by means of mobilisation which in turn requires group consciousness. Finally finance is portrayed as an exponent for what may be termed 'shareholder democracy'. Hence ownership is transferable and so are the rights associated with ownership. Power follows 'matter' rather than individuals and groups. By contrast shopkeepers subscribing to the product market rationale emphasise ownership, albeit they consider it an 'end-goal' rather than a means of control. In sum the four rationales are associated to four different governance ideals: power bargaining, networking, markets and hierarchies accompanied by four corresponding perceived power agencies: social force, control, ownership and citizenship.

Table 2 outlines the four key rationales and their associated 'scores' on central variables such as agents (prime and client), governance ideal and power agency.

*Table 2*

|  | Labour market rationale | Money market rationale | Product market rationale | State power rationale |
|---|---|---|---|---|
| **Bearers –** **prime agents** | Trade unions and employer associations | Central and main commercial banks | Manufacturing and craft-based industry | Ministries of Finance and State |
| **Benefactors** **(clients)** | Unionised workers *(Ministry of Labour)* | International corporate sector *(Ministry of Industry)* | Domestic SMEs *(Market Monitors e.g. Trust Busting Agencies)* | Professions and public sector employees *(Parliament)* |
| **Governance ideal** | Bargaining | Network | Market | Hierarchy |
| **Power agency** | Social force | Control | Ownership | Citizenship |

Dominance by a given rationale inform and bias discourses on political and economic issues including articulated policies with regard to regional integration. Individual political economies reflect a mix of rationales.

Rationale dominance reflects in states' conduct of international relations. This may be true of the style employed vis-à-vis other states and the character of policies advanced. The impact of state action on the international arena is partly dependent on the degree of coherence exhibited. States displaying high levels of diachronic coherence would typically prove a quite enduring platform for international discursive struggles of a domestically dominant rationale. Yet the real time international impact of rationales dominating states possessing great synchronic coherence is likely to be greater.

While rationales associated to the three market categories outlined above and the state have to co-exist in Western economic systems, the institutional component of individual rationales are subject to colonisation from other rationales.

## 4.1   Towards the Social Dimension

In the next chapter the empirical studies are commenced by an analysis of the institutional backdrop framing the EU's social dimension. Developments in key member states and the Brussels level are investigated employing the conceptual framework presented.

Three cases will provide the empirical base for this study. The social dimension is closely associated to one of the four basic freedoms spelled out in the Treaty of Rome. Although labour migration between member states is modest, substantial energy has been invested in erecting a European level body of legislation ensuring wage earners social protection. The political process in connection with the adoption of and the substance in both the 'Framework Directive on Health and Safety' and the 'Maternity Directive' are analysed in chapter 3. Chapter 4 examines the Social Dialogue along similar lines in an historical analysis of the institutional development. Methodologically the cases are approached in a qualitative manner. Chapter 5 seeks to elaborate on the overall dynamics of EU labour market integration and assess the impact on future political initiatives under the social dimension.

# 2 The Institutional Frame: from National Welfare to the EU Social Dimension

## 1 INTRODUCTION

This chapter opens my analysis on the political economy of European labour market integration. What are the issues at stake in relation to the EU's social dimension? At one level they address the questions of the distribution of welfare in society. While integration is instigated in anticipation of welfare gains, the net positive effects of integration are usually not Pareto-optimal. The beneficial effects of increased *intra*-industry trade may thus be countered by welfare losses suffered by particular firms or even regions due to increased *inter*-industry trade. A lack of social and redistributive measures to counter the allocational effects of European integration may cause alarming disparities between regions and citizens grouping them as either winners or losers. This may severely erode public support and hence the legitimacy of the entire venture. At a macro-level a social dimension may thus be designed to alleviate dislocated regions or perhaps even dislocated segments of the work force.[53]

At another level the labour market is a key component of the overall political economic system. Controlling it politically may decisively enhance the governance capacity of central authorities. In addition the institutional feature of core political economic components such as labour markets fundamentally affects the ability of national economies to generate growth and cope with the challenges of structural change. This aspect of the social dimension is what concerns us here.

National economic performance varies between countries beyond what can merely be attributed to differences in factor endowments. This difference reflects corresponding variations in the dynamics of national markets. Market dynamics are determined by institutions governing the economy.[54] Key institutions brings order and recurrence to the apparatus of state, the financial system and the industrial relations system.[55]

38

Institutions can be designed, hence policy makers have some scope for choice in adopting a strategy for national economic development.[56] With the adoption of the internal market, a bias was laid out in Europe's regional institutional configuration. The institutional bias of the internal market scheme is aligned to the 'pure' market rationale associated with neoclassical economics.

The social dimension aims to counter this bias by introducing a substantial system of labour market regulation on the supranational level. Struggles over the design of this decisive institutional feature of the political economic system has become the European Union's most heated battlefield. And it should be!

The institutional design of the EU's social dimension thus determines whether a political capacity for macro-control of one of the two major factor inputs of modern economies will be available for Europe's policy makers. This political control may in turn affect the availability of regional societal mobilisation and consensus formation mechanisms which has served the Union's most successful national economies well.

Likewise, regional labour market prerogatives could prove decisive for the maintenance of the status quo in present national power distributions. A failure to uphold these could result in an institutionally underpinned – but not necessarily broadly desired – dismantling of the regimes ensuring existing welfare systems.

Hence the social dimension concerns the modes and effects of societal governance. The institutional bias of the social dimension is likely to affect the sort of choices made by policy makers, and the action of policy makers operating in a political economic environment conferring on them a degree of governance capacity, is certain to affect the generation and distribution of welfare in society.

While the European Union provides an institutional setting affecting national markets, developments at the European level cannot be understood separately from events in key member states. Although – as shall be discussed later – the EU displays autonomous institutional capabilities enabling it to contribute independently to the shaping of markets, the supranational bearers of European-level institutional properties are severely constrained in their actions by countries such as Germany, France and the United Kingdom. Major integrative steps, such as the internal markets scheme and a fully implemented social dimension, requires support from at least a majority of the most influential members.

National developments determines which policy areas are

considered suitable for joint action. In addition national developments decisively influence the character of joint initiatives. Hence the
social dimension must be understood against the backdrop of changes
in national welfare regimes following the oil crises. Domestic welfare
systems were shaped in power struggles pitting contending rationales
against one another. Although the external pressure generated by the
world recession in the seventies prompted political changes against
established welfare systems across the continent, the direction of
change in individual countries varied considerable due to differences
in national institutional configurations.

In section 2 and accompanying sub-sections national developments
are tracked. National strategies for coping with challenges to the
operating political-economic configurations are examined. Changes
in growth and distribution regimes – the welfare state – are explained
employing the conceptual framework presented in chapter 1.

Section 3 and associated sub-sections probe into the character and
institutional properties of the formal and informal bodies of the
European Union. The Brussels arena is conceptualised vis-à-vis the
understanding of states and markets offered in chapter 1. Finally
section 4 summarises the institutional frame providing the setting for
the making of the European Union's social dimension.

## 2   THE INSTITUTIONAL UNDERPINNING OF NATIONAL WELFARE SYSTEMS

Uncovering the institutional underpinning of national welfare
systems is closely aligned to efforts explaining their emergence. As
the making of welfare states is intertwined with increased public
spending, the formally two separate issues of public spending and
welfare state expansion tend to overlap.

The linkage between these two issues can historically be traced
back to German economist Adolf Wagner's article entitled 'The
Nature of Fiscal Economy' from 1883. Wagner's law simply states that
the pressure for social progress will increase with the general level of
prosperity as demands for social services and the willingness to pay
taxes are income-elastic. At the time of writing the German economy
was experiencing rapid growth following massive industrialisation.[57]
Other functional explanations of the link between industrialisation
and welfare state development point to the efficiency gains in profes-
sionalising welfare services thus ultimately leaving them subject to

productivity levels similar to those of manufacturing industry. Increased efficiency of the 'reproductive' functions would thus be required as industrialisation and rising welfare needs delude households of their ability to perform reproduction in a traditional manner.

Walther Korpi and Gøsta Esping-Andersen have both jointly and individually conducted a series of studies where political coalition making at the national level is regarded as the key to understanding both the extent to which welfare states have developed and the form they have taken. Their explanation for the emergence of welfare states stress the coming into power by the elite's proneness for policies favourable to the working class.

Finally a tradition has developed around the work of Thedda Skocpol stressing the importance of the apparatus of state in the forming of welfare systems. The character of states thus determine the extent to which countries are prone to developing elaborate state sponsored, or state monitored, welfare schemes.

Esping-Andersen and Skocpol are paying allegiance to respectively the labour market and the state power rationale. Wagner's belief in the superior intelligence of market mechanism – exemplified in his comfort with arguments such as 'the price elasticity' of welfare – may tempt contemporary observers to group him with the pure market rationale. Yet the functional logic implied in Wagner, and additionally emphasised in the 'efficiency' perspective as outlined above, bears witness to a *gemeinschaft* perception of society commonly associated to German social thought. The ideals identified with this intellectual current find its contemporary counterpart in the money market rationale.

National institutional configurations are informed by contending rationales. Political struggles on large scale institutional re-configuration, as witnessed with the erection of welfare states, are thus primarily fought out between contending rationales.

In countries like Germany, Britain and France states are, to a varying degree, attributed the establishment of elaborate welfare systems. While states, and the state power rationale, performed pivotal tasks in the making of all three national systems, the room left for contending spheres – and their associated rationales – differed markedly. This decisively affected the resultant institutional configuration of the French, British and German welfare state. In the following sub-sections the institutional underpinning of the welfare state in France, Britain and Germany is explored. Recent developments in the national political economies which either have, or may, affect the future direction of change in domestic welfare systems, are furthermore discussed.

## 2.1   France: Welfare State or State Welfare?

Observers on the history of French social policy frequently point to the devastating effects of military campaigns on the country's demographic composition. Lavish family allowances are accordingly provided as an incentive for the citizens to refurbish the national stock of potential servicemen. In particular World War I laid the foundation for what was to develop later into a full-blown welfare state. The linkage of future state security and elaborate social provisions illustrate the institutional disposition of the French model rather well. It furthermore bears witness to the limited societal embeddedness of a system which otherwise caters rather generously for its citizens.

Following Toqueville the centralised French state left by 18th century absolutism hampered the development of societal counterforces framing contending rationales. Hence 19th century France was prone to recurrent periods of bureaucratic domination punctuated by episodic rebellions.[58] Breaking out of this vicious circle of bureaucratic domination and episodic rebellions required an attempt to decentralise state authority (as the French socialist governments attempted during 1981–86) and to encourage group formation and competition. However, the existing cycle of a centralised state has produced micro-level institutions – habits of thought – sustaining the operations of the central state apparatus.[59]

French society accords a pivotal policy role to administrative elites. High level administrators are the relatives and friends of business and social elites. They come from similar backgrounds.[60] By virtue of socialisation in the best schools they are assured access to the approved universities which stamp them as potential cadres of the ruling class. Elite cadres are selected by their predecessors from the same educational institutions.[61]

A matrix of interrelated state bureaucracies constitute the discourse articulating focal points in the French political economy from which interpreting actors such as labour and for that matter banks and businesses take bearing. Little counterbalance is provided by advocates of contending rationales. While the socialist government attempted to upgrade the negotiated element in the French political economy by strengthening the relative position of labour in the first half of the eighties, trade unions have remained weak and lost 'market shares'. This can be attributed to the approach employed by the state in pushing forward this severe institutional re-configuration. New labour laws were thus passed enhancing the rights of all workers be they organised or not. This illustrates an important dilemma facing states attempting to nurture contending rationales; in that process they have to escape their own institutionally embedded interpretations of governance and power. In granting all workers the same rights the French state maintained its commitment to citizenship. All French subjects are thus covered by this piece of codified regulation designed in the universalistic tradition of 'code Napoleon' – even though this evidently worked contrary to the intention of strengthening the position of *organised* labour.

Trade union coherence was simultaneously attempted by engaging in a 'social dialogue' at the national level which only estranged rank and file members of trade unions and prohibited expansion of the member base as the negotiations concerned abstract issues of macroeconomy, the state was in addition in a much too strong bargaining position vis-à-vis labour to signal the ideal image of a balanced relationship.

Likewise the French currency crisis in the early eighties prompted a new commitment of the French state to monetary stability. With the adoption of the Maastricht treaty the contours of a (designed) money market rationale can be identified as the central bank has been granted formal autonomy. Substantial efforts are thus made to maintain the value of the Franc and meeting EMU convergence criteria. Again, however, these efforts seem to be in vain. Basically the French state is constrained by an institutionally embedded path dependency as its actions reflect its belief in top-down governance even when trying to nurture bottom-up initiated change and a broadened societal underpinning.

This poses serious problems facing the state when trying to design the base for a contending rationale. Hence the lack of a broad institutional underpinning hampers the ability to establish a society-wide understanding of the character of problems countered and the available set of solutions. The discourse-formative capacity of a state designed base of political action, with little or no societal rooting is extremely limited.[62] Toqueville's observations on episodic rebellions is a reflection of this problem which is additionally illustrated with recent strikes prompted by economic reforms informed by the money market rationale. A system ensuring an acceptable distribution of costs and benefits of changes endured by a dramatic re-orientation of policy priorities may alleviate some of the problems, but eventually even such a system requires broad legitimacy in the form of fundamental institutional features stressing consensus, cooperation and societal needs as any distribution relies on compromises and consequently rarely conforms to Pareto-optimal allocation functions.

French networks are formed by individuals but these are subject to a political culture of a Gemeinschaft nature applying universalistic norms of behaviour. This network culture is nurtured by the educational system and refined by the grand corps structure which overrules formal network relations organised on the basis of functional lines.

To sum up, state attempts to form a base for the labour and money market rationale has largely failed. Changes can, however, be observed in the French political economy. Some movements towards the erection of a product market rationale is thus witnessed by the de-nationalisation of large firms and the country's cordial acceptance and fairly thorough implementation of the EU's internal market. The political aspirations of the French state has, however, been to advance bases for contending rationales in a manner which does not result in the replacement of state power by market power. While the market has been attempted to be upgraded the bases of a genuine product market rationale has not been subject to an active construction process as seen in the cases of labour and money. Although French compliance with internal market regulations is fairly good, the commitment on behalf of the French state with regard to this project has characteristically not been fully extended to the vital element of public procurement.

The transition from a state rationale to a product market rationale is fairly easy as it involves less explicit use of bottom-up dynamics. Less state under such conditions – given no effective base for contending rationales is in operation – will inevitably produce more market. This potential ease of transition has been a key motivation behind state attempts to nurture bases for contending rationales. While market efficiency has increasingly been deemed a desirable output of policies on institutional change by the French state, a fully fledged product market rationale is regarded as least compatible with the institutionally founded preferences of the elite.

European integration is both regarded as a source and vehicle of change. The product market rationale of the internal market scheme thus alerted the base of the French state rationale of its fragility in the face of globalisation. Consequent attempts of erecting counter-institutions of social dialogue and negotiated money market management has been directed both at the domestic level and – at French insistence – at the European level.

## 2.2 Great Britain: From Welfare to Workfare

Academic accounts on British socioeconomic history – from Friedrich Engles to Richard Titmuss – has traditionally stressed the pervasive impacts of commodification on the living conditions among the least privileged members of society. Pure markets ideals acquired a solid hold of the UK's political economy. Possibly induced by the liberal operating environment offered by institutional features such as the principle of 'common law', industrialisation took off in this country before anywhere else paving the way for new – highly flexible – ideals on transaction: the pure market. We may speculate that the rather unique system of 'common law' emerged because state development and the social constitution of nationhood, unlike the French experience, was roughly concurrent. It certainly seems likely that under a 'common law' regulatory framework barriers to bottom-up market development, that is, the guild system and royal charters and so on, could be easier bypassed by imaginative entrepreneurs than under a 'Roman law' regime.

Britain was the cradle for both trade unionism and the modern welfare state. The former took off as the process of industrialisation peaked. The latter was founded on the rubbles of the blitz. Although English workers won hard fought concessions in numerous industrial action, government initially maintained an arms-length attitude to the industrial relations system. Britain's industrial relations system was thus notorious for its lack of a coherent system of labour codes even during the heyday of welfare statism.

State-sponsored welfare policy in the immediate post-war era thus bypassed the industrial relations system. Institutionally this resulted in a weak linkage between the institutionalised preferences of unions acquired through the social practice of collective bargaining and industrial action, and the echelons of state power elites moulding the new welfare regime. While the latter took bearing from the former, they failed to discard institutional leftovers from previously dominant rationales. The labour market rationale never fully settled as ideals derived of both the pure market and the state power sphere proved too ingrained in the nation's political economic configuration. This spilled back to the trade union movement. Accordingly the shop steward institution has commonly been dismissed as too pragmatic and not sufficiently geared towards assuring fundamental changes on the labour market.

The Beveridge welfare model implemented following the Second World War, essentially provide for minimum benefits allowing recipients to survive economic downturns. Unlike the corporatist models of Germany and France, which allow dislocated workers to at least temporarily maintain earned privileges in terms of, for example, higher pay obtained while on the labour market, the British system only assures a possible market re-entrance of unemployed workers at concurrent terms. In this sense it supports the pure market ideals entrenched in the UK labour market rather than seeking to alter its institutional properties.

In short the labour market rationale never fully penetrated industrial relations as contending rationales drawing on state power and pure market ideals provided a counter-force. Creating the base for a labour market rationale was thus a key priority in the seventies. This proved highly counter-productive to the Labour Party administration as the fragmentation of the craft-based trade union movement made it impossible to implant a common sense of purpose onto it.

The relative ease with which the Conservative administration eradicated the influence of organised labour in less than a decade illustrates the situation well. This was only possible because there was an alternative discourse upon which competing ideals could be articulated. The failure of Labour governments in establishing a working societal governance system while in majority, similarly illustrates the fragility faced by the labour market sphere and its associated rationale.

Britain's welfare state is consequently too much state – and the labour market too much market. Neither welfare state nor labour market found refuge in the labour market rationale which likewise failed to form the common ground linking the two spheres in a workable societal governance platform.

Conditions for a money market rationale, however, appear somewhat more promising. On the surface the Bank of England has certainly in the past been regarded as a hallmark of monetary stability and while free-floating exchange rates was a distinctive feature of Thatcherite economic policy, so also was continuous – usually futile – attempts to control the money supply and thus counter inflation. In addition the UK's industry structure bears some resemblance to that of Germany in that a few major banks dominate the market and the corporate sector is the most concentrated in the OECD. Large commercial banks and large firms are thus plentiful and as a strong central bank is in operation all necessary ingredients are present for a money market rationale.

But British banks and industrial firms have traditionally co-existed and co-operated on market terms rather than embarking in more intimate relationships. One reason is the intermediary function of the country's large and well-functioning stock exchange. In the world of market-led finance, firms are commodities which are traded in the same way as oil, currencies and wheat!

Another reason is the institutional features relating to the operation of networks. Great Britain exhibits network relations subject to a political culture featuring individuals joining in Geselschaft-type relations applying particularistic norms of behaviour. This makes for enormous complexity for banks wanting to conduct business with a broad range of customers in an intimate network manner. Relations therefore succumb – or degenerate – into standard operating procedures mastered by all participants namely rule-wise transparent exchange relations between optimising agents.

Great Britain has experienced the fiercest battles on welfare system design in post-war Europe. On the balance the broader welfare state has remained true to its founding principles. Hence social benefits are still allotted on a minimum – often means-tested – basis. Similarly the welfare system in operation functions separately to the industrial relations system which has deteriorated signficantly since the showdown between the state and organised labour in the eighties. Employers have all but abandoned collective bargaining, and British elites apparently seem to consider the free market of Europe, rather than the potential joint regulatory capacity of Europe, as their future source of welfare.

## 2.3   Germany: Welfare Society Postponed?

Although the German nation preceded the German state, a state initiated welfare system was introduced in Germany by Otto von Bismarck roughly at the same time Disraeli proposed his social measure to the House of Commons. Besides timing, early welfare state development the UK and Germany share the feature that state sponsored social provisions were launched by patriarchal conservative rulers fearing social unrest in the wake of rapid urbanisation and rampant industrialisation.

Yet important differences overshadow the similarities. In the realm of production, German industrialisation preceded the creation of a comprehensive market system. Institutionally the employment contracts of state-induced industrial enterprises catering for government demands, took bearing from the only labour market in operation: the civil service. Hence due to the state-led industrialisation process, contract based employment was introduced in Germany before market ideals had acquired a firm grip of the nation's political economy.

Unlike France, German state-sponsored industrialisation did not pave the way for state power dominance. First, post-1871 German statehood at least formally cherished decentralisation since the country was an amalgamation of several duchies. Secondly, national sentiments had nourished the state-creation process all along pointing to the desirability of uniting the German nation which was in fact doing rather well in spite of political-administrative fragmentation. In sum, the German state could not make claim to have created the German nation – as is the case of France.

Although remarkably tolerant of deviant regional practices, the imperial German state was a slow starter with regards to democracy. The struggle for parliamentary government was spearheaded by the social democratic party – unlike Britain where the battle had been fought out earlier and between contenders from different spheres. Traditional 'burgher' revolutions had been ignited in several of the smaller German duchies from the late 1830s and onwards. However, with the establishment of the imperial constitutional order in the wake of the 1871 Franco-German war, the traditional vanguard of liberal revolutions gradually started to lose ground. Labour organisers in association with the revisionist German social democratic party became the decisive force in the struggle for parliamentary government. Starting with the military barrack rebellions of late World War I, the labour market rationale made important inroads in the state sphere peaking with the ill-fated Weimar republic.

A strong money market rationale was embedded in the constitution of the Federal Republic as the Central Bank was accorded unprecedented autonomy. The micro-foundations was already in place as the 'Hausbank' concept and the dominance of the 'big three' had been established prior to the war.[63] This has partially been counter-balanced by a fairly strong labour market rationale which was underpinned by the access granted to corporate boardrooms of labour representatives by the administrations of the occupying forces. The reconstruction of the pre-nazi era labour movement, greatly enhanced the capacity of the political economy to link externally conferred workers' rights to an endogenously moulded labour market rationale.

From the late sixties up through the seventies labour enjoyed support from governments with either social democratic leadership or participation. This produced a near match between the labour and money market rationales. Yet with the de facto installation of the Deutschmark as the European core currency in connection with the introduction of the ERM in 1979, and a change of government, labour was increasingly on the retreat. It has often been attempted to counter this, lately with the futile initiative of IG Metal in spring 1996.

An essential outcome of money market dominance is the position of private banks as network nodes in relation to both economic policy and commercial market operations. The elevation of German banks to their present position in the conduct of societal management has of course been assisted by basic institutional properties of the country's economy. The organic German network tradition prompt firms to regard bank capital as quasi-endogenous simply because manufacturers and bankers are subject to a joint sense of purpose. Consequently networks are fairly easily re-configured along functional lines. The network tradition is underpinned by societal features of a Gemeinschaft-type featuring an application of universalistic norms of behaviour.

Hence Germany's welfare state rests both on the money and the labour market rationale. Establishing trust between employers and employees remains the discursive frame of reference for all 'responsible' socioeconomic actors. This finds its most vivid expression in the vocational training system and the participation of labour representatives in firm management. Welfare provisions are largely administrated through semi-autonomous contribution-based schemes, operating on the money market in order to maintain or expand equity.

## 2.4 Welfare States, Labour Markets and Regional Integration

National welfare states are shaped by the overall domestic institutional configuration. Indeed national welfare regimes constitute the institutional configuration. Modes for generating and distributing welfare essentially define the character of domestic political economies.

National welfare models have evolved in response to power struggles between contending rationales. Historical circumstances, such as the timing of state formation vis-à-vis industrialisation and the social constitution of nationhood cast particular biases into the initial institutional frame.

Early nationhood in combination with late state formation may assure the latter a high degree of societal embeddedness. Institutionally the state power sphere may as a consequence partially adopt pre-modern organic prescriptions on transaction and governance. As spheres spouting transaction ideals based on new social practices emerge, corresponding rationales may plug into compatible institutional properties rooted in the pre-modern order. This would seem to be the case with Germany's money and labour market rationale.

Early state formation and late nationhood may on the other hand produce an institutional configuration leaving preciously little room for pre-modern prescriptions. Rather 'modern' governance ideals are likely to permeate the state sphere. Limited societal embeddedness may produce 'missionary' state behaviour causing colonisation attempts in the realm of labour, money and product markets. This is evident in the contemporary French political economy.

Concurrent emergence of nationhood and statehood is likely to result in an institutional order where divergent social practices can co-exist. Flexibility in the fundamental set of rules overseeing governance and transaction might conceivably prevail – as in the principle of common law. Britain would seem to fit this prescription.

Subsequent national developments are locked into particular trajectories leaving room for power struggles between different spheres informed by, and advancing, corresponding rationales. The timing of industrialisation – and the accompanying advance of market ideals – in relation to state formation and the social constitution of nationhood, comprise an example of a protracted historical factor affecting the ensuing balance between rationales. In sum, the historical sequence of respectively state formation, the social constitution of nationhood and industrialisation, determines how key West European political economies are institutionally configured. The basic historical-institutional imprints left on these systems are reproduced in welfare state designs.

Germany's welfare state is perhaps best described as a con-societal corporatist model. The social partners enjoy significant state autonomy, social provisions are administered by foundations subject to both labour market and money market virtues. The federal state and individual Länder monitor the arrangement in a regulatory capacity.

Recent changes have caused the money market rationale to gain ground, but the overall operation of the system has not been fundamentally altered.

France's welfare system is intrinsically statist. It can appropriately be denoted a state-centred corporatist model. The autonomy of the social partners in dealing with labour market issues is at a minimum. Social provisions are administered by state bodies or formally independent organisations effectively functioning as clients of the Paris bureaucracy. Recent changes have seen futile attempts on the part of the state to construct the foundation for contending spheres in the realm of labour and the money market. In sum the French state has actively pursued strategies of political economic institutional reconfiguration in the face of problems perceived as structural. This has made the institutional configuration of this country's welfare regime very volatile in the period subject to scrutiny. Erecting a European welfare system has been identified as one possible response to current French problems, making this member state a key actor in relation to the spectacle surrounding the social dimension.

Lord Beveridge headed the commission drawing up basic principles for Britain's post-war welfare state. 'The Beveridge model' has since come to denote a state-centred system allowing for significant municipal discretion. It in addition implies a delinkage of the industrial relations system from the bodies providing social services and benefits. To the extent that an interplay can be identified between social provisions and the labour market, it is in the implicit amplification of pure market traits provided by the former in the realm of the latter.

The labour market rationale in particular tried to make its weight felt in domestic power struggles up through the seventies. With the conservative administration taking office in 1979 a counter-offensive was successfully launched. Although painful the ensuing struggle was easily won as the market rationale was deeply entrenched in virtually all spheres of the UK's political economy. The labour market rational never gained a firm hold of the British welfare state and the institutional configuration still conforms to the Beveridge model. Changes can, however, be observed because the labour market sphere is increasingly subject to colonisation by the pure market rationale.

The above outline of national configurational changes in the welfare arrangement of key member states form the stage for the struggle over the European Union's social dimension. In particular France has, on the backdrop of severe challenges to the domestic order, sought to enrol the European level. French elites strive to found a system of welfare generation, distribution and governance not succumbing to the pure market rationale, but nonetheless compatible with global political-economic developments. Germany has certainly informally provided a point of reference for segments of the French elite. So has Britain, but in a rather negative sense.

The latter country stands out as the main opponent to a European social dimension. This country has found comfort in a political economic system according relative hegemony to the pure market rationale. Contending spheres have found themselves on the most pervasive retreat since World War I.

Germany does not have much of a strategy in the field, but is institutionally biased towards the French position with regard to the desired end-state rather than the method conceived. The problem is that Germany would not know how to politically construct a political setting imitating its own institutional properties in the welfare domain. The bottom-up dynamics of the German system relies on societal embeddedness and a capacity for mutual learning not attainable in a joint European setting within a foreseeable future. Hence the substance of Franco-German differences on the matter relate partly to urgency – it is France who is perceived to be in need of an immediate institutional overhaul – and partly methodology.

Evidently member states are not the only actors in the EU. Bodies such as the European Commission, the European Parliament etc. play important roles. But do they host strategies? Can they act as bearers of particular rationales, and do they display sufficient coherence to advance policies embodying institutionalised ideals on governance and transaction?

## 3   THE SUPRANATIONAL CONTEXT FOR LABOUR MARKET INTEGRATION

The characteristics of the EU, with its blend of federalism, confederalism and genuine intergovernmentalism, and the consequent effects on actor participation and behaviour, highlight three features separating it from national systems. The first and most widely recognised is the inaccessibility of organised interest to the most central policy-makers at the supranational level (for example, the Council of Ministers). The second is the diminishing role of the electorate. There is thus no common European public opinion aggregated into

European-wide party platforms and subsequently transformed into policies in powerful, directly elected policy making bodies. The third is the limited scope of the EU in comparison with states.

Employing a state analogy thus poses considerable problems. Yet the very fact that a directly elected Parliament exists, and that it seemingly has been gaining power in the last two decades, suggests that the European Union's political system is more than an international organisation but less than a confederation.

The term supranational is often employed to imply that it is the EU level as opposed to the national level which is the locus of inquiry. Yet according to Ernst Haas the term:

> [R]efers to a process or style of decision-making, 'a cumulative pattern of accommodation in which the participants refrain from unconditionally vetoing proposals and instead seek to attain agreement by means of compromises upgrading common interest'.[64]

While the Council is recognised as the central forum of decision making a broader policy-making process involving a multitude of actors precedes the high level deliberation between ministers. It is a central claim by proponents of the supranational perspective that these sub-Council fora deserve substantial academic attention.

The supranational understanding of the EU's policy-making process has chiefly been identified with the *neo-functionalist* body of thinking. Neo-functionalism predicts that European integration will be a step by step process, in sharp opposition to conventional international relations theory which focus on crises rather than incremental change. Neo-functionalism rests on pluralist democratic theory which is essentially 'state-less'. Consequently little attention is devoted to assessing the character of the EU vis-à-vis states and international organisations. The most lucid statement on the character of the EU level organisations offered by neo-functionalism is the notion of institutional spillover.[65] It is thus contended that in particular the Commission of the European Union (CEU), but also other EU bodies, are infused with a sense of purpose which is inherently pro-integrationist. A natural bias informs the organisations when designing, proposing and implementing EU policies. Problems are accordingly identified and analysed in a manner favouring 'European' rather than national solutions. Policies tend to be maximalists to the extent this is compatible with the political climate in the Council.

Pluralism, and hence neo-functionalism, are essentially elitist theories. Socialisation processes, as implied in political spillover, is solely applicable to elites. In this study social embeddedness is stressed. Elites are evidently socialised and institutionalise common understandings in terms of causal beliefs, appropriateness and purpose. Supranationality as defined by Ernst Haas is an example of institutionalised elite ideals and patterns of behaviour socially created by means of interaction between pioneer elite segments and subsequently disseminated and reproduced by means of socialisation. Supranational as defined by Ernst Haas thus constitutes an institutionalised 'logic of appropriateness' and hence is a source of autonomy. But can, for example, the Commission act autonomously vis-à-vis other actors and the constituent civil societies, and to what extent does the Brussels level exhibit coherence and unity of action? How can the issue of embeddedness be handled in relation to the EU hybrid? And finally, do the EU bodies display a specific sense of purpose reflected in the process of institutional spillover? These questions will be examined following the introduction of the actors in the European level labour market policy arena.

## 3.1    The Council

Following the institutional logic of the EU, the Council is the supreme decision-making body entrusted with the task of passing EU legislation. It is assisted by the COREPER which prepares the agenda of the Council. Proposals for EU legislation are made by the CEU which in the process consults extensively with a number of advisory and management committees. At some point in the negotiation process between the Council and the CEU arising from the above-mentioned division of labour, the European Parliament and the Economic and Social Committee (ESC) has to be consulted on the legislation under consideration. Although the above outline of the EU policy process is crude it does capture the basic principles.

The Social Policy Council – convening national ministers of labour – meets between two and three times a year. The frequency of meetings has gone up since the introduction of the Social Action Programme and is likely to increase even further as the more extensive provisions of the Maastricht Treaty's Social Protocol comes into force.

COREPER is the workhorse of the Council. It seats the permanent representative of the member states but due to the sheer size of its work load it has had to split into two and in addition form some 130 working groups. COREPER I and II divide the tasks between them even though the ambassadors in COREPER I assume responsibilities of all matters handled in the realm of COREPER. Social policy is in the purview of COREPER II and as such is deemed one of the Union's less prestigious policy areas.

The European Council was formally established by a treaty amendment in 1974. In practice it had been in operation since the 1969 Hague Summit. Bringing together the heads of government and the French head of state at least twice a year, it functions as a board of directors for the Union. Its role is primarily to act in an overall agenda setting capacity.

While the Council undoubtedly has socialising effects on its members, the proposition advanced by, in particular, neo-functionalist scholars, stating that ministers and their officials do not merely act as national agents but are, by means of frequent Council sessions, gradually socialised into thinking on a European-wide scale, is both crucial and controversial. The Council is recognised as the EU venue where national interests may be legitimately promoted. Yet the institution of supranationality as identified by Haas refers to a mode of Council deliberation which is distinctly non-intergovernmental.

Frequent use of package strategies nonetheless points to the significance of national interests in Council bargaining. The Council hierarchy placing the Foreign Minister at the top signals that the vanguard of states in international affairs may still monopolise 'national interest' in civilian power settings such as the EU. On the other hand, the implied issue-linkage is evidence of an opening of national societies – the sheltering of which has constituted the *raison d'être* of Foreign Ministries in the first place. The institution of issue-linking also reflects the commitment of states to operate within the confinement of the EU framework even though this means compromising sovereignty in areas not intended as objects for cooperation. Finally, issue-linkage provides coordination to an otherwise highly sectorised policy setting and hence implant an element of coherence.

Some clear-cut cases of deep EU resentment among political elites from influential member states has had significant impact on the workings of the Council and hence the development of the Union. States exhibiting considerable diachronic coherence while constrained by synchronic incoherence may severely disrupt the workings of the Council but are usually subject to long-term exhaustion caused by isolation and hence likely to eventually fall back in line with other states. Such states may in addition be more susceptible to the socialising effects of EU participation than states firmly embedded in their domestic societies. States objecting to further integration and at the same time displaying synchronic coherence may constitute a more enduring problem for the pro-integration stance. As argued in chapter 1, states firmly embedded in their domestic societies rarely boast highly centralised state apparatuses. Opposition from such states may consequently take on a more benevolent nature and the disruptive effects on Council workings appear less severe.

Simultaneously functioning as venue and actor is not exclusive to the Council. Parliaments frequently find themselves in a similar position. While MPs have distinct constituencies warranting specific interests, parliaments as a whole are in some instances regarded as autonomous actors. Neo-corporatist arrangements thus work detrimental to the inherent interests of parliaments as they transfer political power from the legislative to the executive. Similarly the Council possess autonomy vis-à-vis other formal EU organisations but not necessarily member states. As other formal EU organisations have gained influence due to either leadership – CEU under Delors – or constitutional upgrades – the European Parliament and the European Court of Justice following Maastricht – institutional adhesion has increased, reinforcing the actor trait of the Council at the expense of the venue trait. This may strengthen the 'sense of purpose' yielding institutional spillover mechanisms which previously have been identified primarily with the CEU and the ECJ.

Council operations are qualified by institutions such as supranationality. It exhibits some coherence of action vis-à-vis other actors but is at the same time a legitimate venue for opposing interests. As a supranational entity the Council combines elements from states and venues of international cooperation. A crucial factor distinguishing the Council from states is the complete lack of societal embeddedness. No facility for interest intermediation thus ensures the conveying of specific societal preferences other than the states themselves. Furthermore no general public exhibiting common cultural features underpin Council discourse, yet other political systems function while serving culturally highly diversified societal basis, but unlike the Council they are not challenged and colonised by fairly coherent states displaying substantial, though varying, degrees of embeddedness.

## 3.2   The Commission of the European Union (CEU)

Formally the initiator of Union policies, the CEU assumes a central role in all European level policy making. Besides acting as the executive assigned with implementing EU law the CEU in addition has been labelled the guardian of the treaties. CEU is the 'engine' of integration as it is the only authority endowed with the privilege of drafting EU legislation.

General Directorate number five – or DGV – is in charge of the EU's social and labour market policy. As at the time of writing the Commissioner responsible for these matters is Irish national Padraig Flynn. For the period under survey DGV was headed first by Manuel Marin of Spain and later Vasso Papandraeus of Greece.[66]

The CEU displays certain organisational traits constituting a hindrance to efficient administrative and policy-making performance. These can be divided into three categories: (1) patterns of recruitment and personnel policy; (2) the structure of the internal organisation; and (3) coordination problems caused by lacking budgetary and financial instruments.

For our purpose problems associated to the structure and internal organisation of the CEU are of particular relevance. It is thus a source of fragmentation resulting in both lack of policy coherence and professional inequality. The professional level of the CEU is thus being asserted differently in different sectors by national bureaucracies. While the 'Directorate Generale' (DG) dealing with agriculture generally commands respect among national Ministries of Agriculture, the DG assigned to social and labour market policy – DG number five (DGV) – is regarded somewhat less respectfully by its national counterparts. Likewise DGV is generally not subject to high esteem by national labour market organisation.

Although originally conceived as a relatively small body directed by a college of Commissioners, the structure of the CEU has proliferated. The structure of DGs displays vertical divisions with rigid demarcation lines hampering cross-compartmental communications and consequently coordination. The administration of the specialised units has demanded a growing amount of the individual Commissioner's attention and turned them into 'policy specialists'. This makes the college of Commissioners less of a collective entity since the coherent appearance of the CEU is easily undermined as no ideological ties bind the Commissioners together.

Finally, the CEU is continuously subject to organisational checks as successive enlargements require the absorption of hundreds of new officials unaccustomed with EU procedures while often deeply entrenched in domestic administrative cultures.

Constituting a comprehensive bureaucratic system the CEU boasts little in the way of cultural embeddedness. While displaying strong leadership in the form of an executive acting in a coherent manner, officials of the CEU conduct bureaucratic government with substantial discretion. Due to the vast amount of external contacts nurtured and the sheer size of the CEU, top-down governance as exercised by the executive is bound to have a limited impact. The CEU thus interacts extensively with political and economic elites throughout Europe. The CEU – in accordance with neo-functional prescriptions – aims to compensate for lacking cultural embeddedness by seeking contacts with European elites representing interests affected by EU policy.

Only European associations have direct and formal contacts with the CEU.[67] This applies only, however, to organisations having received Commission approval.[68] Through its policy of excluding national interest groups from direct and formal access, the CEU actively stimulates formation of European associations. Once created, European associations share fundamental common interests with the CEU as they provide legitimacy and authority to other.

The CEU displays unity of action at the executive level. A particular European 'ideology' has been nurtured by CEU officials and executive adherence to these ideals is likely to enhance synchronic coherence. Yet failure to achieve compatibility between executive values and bureaucratic values on European integration may amplify fragmentation and 'hostile discretion' exercised by the lower echelons. The lack of an external executive power base leaves room for embedded Commission ideology to take hold in the college of Commissioners. Generally speaking the CEU has shown considerable diachronic coherence. What has fluctuated over time is not the CEU's European discourse but rather its impact. The CEU is possibly the most autonomous international bureaucracy of its kind. Member states have installed various checks in the EU framework to control the Commission but essentially the organisation has managed to maintain a high level of sovereignty vis-à-vis the Council. In spite of numerous crises and setbacks the CEU still displays a sense of purpose and thus is a prime cultivator of institutional spillover.

### 3.3   The European Parliament

Two consultative bodies are established by the EU treaties: the Economic and Social Committee (ESC) and the European Parliament (EP). With Maastricht a third body was created representing regional authorities. Formally denoted the Assembly until the 1986 Single European Act (SEA) Treaty revision, the Parliament has slowly evolved beyond merely performing consultative tasks. With Maastricht the EP became what it strived for all along: a European Parliament although it still cannot match the powers of its national counterparts.

Delegates have formed cross-national political groupings, the largest of which are the Socialist and the Christian Democrat formations. Most of the political work is done in one of the 18 sub-committees.

In the pre-Maastricht era, which forms the historical setting for much of this study, the EP had only few serious options for making an impact on EU policy making. The annual budget could be moderately altered by an absolute majority and the college of Commissioners dismissed from office. It was only with the introduction of the SEA cooperation procedure that the EP was granted real powers. According to the cooperation procedure the EP may force the Council to adopt a given piece of internal market (SEM) legislation using a unanimous vote rather than the qualified majority voting procedure otherwise provided for directives and regulations of this nature. This again requires that the EP mobilises an absolute majority and the legislation under consideration falls under the SEM heading.

The EP has managed to fully exploit the limited prerogatives granted with the cooperation procedure. This has led to a rediscovery of this institution among lobbyist and social partners. The Parliament is now a central actor in most aspects of EU social policy making and interchangeably cooperates and competes with the social partners.

In the wake of formal upgrades accompanying SEA and Maastricht, confidence among MEPs is high and reflected in the vigorous advocacy of the 'democracy discourse'. The EP perceives its task as bringing democracy to the peoples of Europe. The legitimacy of the integrative venture is rarely questioned even though a number of parliamentarians are elected on an anti-EU ballot. Both a sense of purpose and features conducive for institutional spillover can thus be identified.

As with the Council, EP operations are marked by the duality of being a legitimate venue for opposing interests and an actor vis-à-vis other bodies. Article 189B of the Maastricht Treaty introduced the Co-Decision Procedure which besides granting the EP a veto in certain policy fields contained provisions for a conciliation committee representing Parliament against the Council. This feature may upgrade the level of coherence in EP dealings and thus reinforce the actor element of this body.[69]

Like the CEU the Parliament displays significant autonomy in its dealings with other formal organisations and member states. In being a supranational entity promoting democracy and openness in an otherwise inaccessible setting, the EP is more attuned to societal preferences than most other bodies which solely take bearing on the basis of elite reference. Still, no general public exhibiting common cultural features underpin EP discourse.

### 3.4  The Social Partners

A number of European associations may be designated 'social partner'. On the side of labour, associations paying allegiance to trade unionism see their task as primarily being to advance the social development of the EU. On the side of employers a highly diverse structure exists. Most groupings representing 'capital' consider themselves business associations promoting the overall conditions of private enterprise at the EU level. In this respect their 'natural' policy realm is industrial policy rather than labour market policy. Some of them consequently refuse to deal with matters concerning the social dimension as it is the case of the well-organised European Chemical Industry Association (CEFIC).

Different incentives separating European level trade unions and employer associations must be appreciated when assessing the commitment of national constituent organisations. Trade unions of a socialist observance basically have an internationalist outlook. They regard cross-national cooperation as valuable in itself. Employers are more instrumental. They basically regard each other as competitors and are reluctant to invest time and money in cross-national cooperation unless tangible results are likely to be produced. While trade unions have had international cooperation since the London Dock Strike in the late 19th century they have been rather slow in developing customised organisations geared at influencing the EU policy process. By contrast, businesses formed European associations specifically with a view to influence all stages of EU policy making.

Umbrella organisations representing the social partners at the EU level are primarily the European Trade Union Confederation (ETUC)[70] and the Union des Industries de la Communauté Européenne (UNICE).[71] Minor organisations on the side of business include the agricultural producers (COPA) and the Centre Européen de l'Entreprise Public (CEEP) organising publicly owned enterprises. The vertical interrelation of the European level social partners does not follow a coherent pattern. As a general rule trade unions seem to display more consistent structures than employer associations.

ETUC, organising white and blue collar workers within all industries, was founded in 1973 on the groundwork of two ideologically competing European confederations.[72] ETUC comprises 39 national trade unions in 21 European countries with a total of 45 million members. This is estimated to encompass about 95 per cent of all unionised workers in the region.

Besides national trade union centres some 15 intermediary and branch level European associations are members of ETUC. This number represents the vast majority of functioning intermediary and branch level labour organisations at the European level.[73]

The founding of ETUC has undoubtedly enhanced labour's influence towards EU bodies, but generally labour is rather weak vis-à-vis in particular the CEU. The very character of the EU can thus be claimed to be biased towards private industry. Consequently the values and preferences of the CEU executive and staff rests rather heavily on free market ideology. As social democracy prevailed in the domestic setting of member states the seventies witnessed the emergence of more radical social policies on the EU agenda. Yet labour still had difficulties in facing the power of European business. Part of the reason is persistent lack of organisational coherence as important national unions – adhering to the Communist brand of trade unionism – until recently remained outside the ETUC. Likewise major member associations such as TUC and the Scandinavian LO's displayed considerable reluctance in their European commitment.

ETUC has commissioned some studies of its relative weakness. Part of the problem seems to be under-funding. A number of national federations are fairly impoverished explaining the rather modest budget of ETUC. In terms of resources ETUC's secretariat is roughly comparable in size with the generally much more successful UNICE, particularly when including the European Trade Union Institute (ETUI) which is the research department of ETUC. This relatively new branch is nearly entirely sponsored by the CEU. Generally speaking it appears the CEU has attempted to level ETUC and UNICE by subsidising the activities of the former such as witnessed in relation to ETUI and the Technical Bureau established in the aftermath of the Machinery Directive.[74]

UNICE, which organises service and manufacturing industries, was founded in 1958. UNICE comprises 32 national industry and employer federations from 22 countries. No European level intermediary and branch level associations are members of UNICE, but national member federations maintain permanent representatives in Brussels. The permanent representatives constitute the core committee of the UNICE organisational framework.

UNICE's relative strength can be explained by strong consensus on policy objectives among national member federations. No clear-cut demarcations as with divergent national patterns of trade unionism can be observed.[75] Spanish employers have thus not developed a special brand of business politicking in response to strong syndicalist traditions in the country's labour movement. UNICE has in addition been assisted in advancing its course by a plethora of intermediary and branch level associations. Large and powerful sectorial associations exists within, for example, chemistry and steel. Since 1983 the European Roundtable of Industrialists, drawing an extremely exclusive membership, has formed a very powerful group aiming at improving overall business conditions for European industry.

When comparing the performance of UNICE with ETUC, differences with regard to their chief task and the environment within which aims are to be accomplished must be taken into account. The fulfilment of UNICE's top priority – the adoption of the internal market scheme – has been assisted by express Treaty reference to these policies which in addition constitute the *raison d'être* of the EU. UNICE does not need to set the agenda but merely lend support and political legitimacy to policies enjoying considerable institutional support. The social dimension, which is not a positive objective of UNICE, has had ETUC as main proponent with occasional backing from individual member states such as France in the eighties. In addition CEU president Jacques Delors offered consistent support but the fact remains that the EU's organisational framework is poorly suited to sustain some of the proposed policies which in addition are challenged on grounds of fundamental soundness by a key member state.

European associations contribute to agenda formation in the EU, but member states and the CEU remain chief contributors in this respect. Once a policy has been initiated, however, there is often a substantial role to be played by the former group of actors. Consequently ETUC has only now been given a chance to prove its worth.

Neither of the main European level social partners appears to posses significant levels of autonomy vis-à-vis member organisations. National affiliates have substantial control of the Brussels offices and often enjoy privileged access to domestic policy settings which may provide blocking of undesired policy outcomes via the Council. According to Philip Schmitter and Wolfgang Streeck employers have deliberately under-organised at the European level in order to avoid being sucked in to a CEU initiated labour market policy spiral.[76] UNICE thus displays coherence by means of a strategy of non-commitment. ETUC is significantly more autonomous in relation to the national constituency than UNICE. Besides allowing for qualified majority voting, leaving more political space for the secretariat, the organisation has managed to get substantial CEU funding. Yet this obviously undermines ETUC autonomy in relation to the Commission. ETUC may thus partially be regarded as a socialisation exercise aimed at national trade unions.

Institutionalised patterns of behaviour can be observed in some of the policy formulating bodies of the social partners. Euro-elites of national organisations display some joint sense of purpose particularly on the side of labour. The European agenda, however, generally enjoys less attention in national trade unions than is the case of business associations and states.

### 3.5 Brussels Between Welfare States and Labour Markets

Previous writings on the character of the EU have been ambiguous. Key terms such as 'socialisation' and 'supranational' extracted from neo-functionalism in conjunction with traditional state virtues such as sovereignty, autonomy and coherence have formed the nexus for our exploration of the nature of the EU versus states and their markets.

In sum, the Council socialise members although the neo-functionalist proposition in this regards needs to be modified. States exhibiting diachronic coherence while constrained by synchronic incoherence may severely disrupt the workings of the Council but are usually subject to long-term exhaustion caused by isolation and hence likely to eventually fall back in line. States opposing integrative measures while displaying synchronic coherence may constitute a more enduring problem for the pro-integration stance.

The Council simultaneously functions as venue and actor causing it to possess autonomy vis-à-vis other formal EU organisations but not necessarily member states. Increased influence gained by other formal EU organisations may strengthen the 'sense of purpose' and hence the practice of institutional spillover.

While the CEU displays strong leadership in the form of an

executive acting in a coherent manner, Commission officials conduct bureaucratic government with substantial discretion in their extensive interaction with political and economic elites. An integration 'ideology' is nurtured by the CEU thus enhancing synchronic coherence making the Commission a prime cultivator of institutional spillover. Incompatibility between executive and bureaucratic values may amplify fragmentation but the CEU has shown considerable diachronic coherence. The CEU is possibly the most autonomous international bureaucracy of its kind maintaining a high level of sovereignty vis-à-vis the Council.

The European Parliament is increasingly confident following constitutional upgrades. It aspires to be the advocate of democracy in the EU system whose basic legitimacy is rarely questioned. Both a sense of purpose and features conducive for institutional spillover are present in this rapidly developing organisation.

European level social partners possess little autonomy vis-à-vis member organisations. UNICE seek to avoid making commitments on labour market policy. This strategy is pursued with some coherence. ETUC has greater autonomy than UNICE. Besides allowing for qualified majority voting the organisation has managed to get CEU funding. This undermines ETUC autonomy vis-à-vis the Commission.

## 4   THE INSTITUTIONAL FRAMING OF THE SOCIAL DIMENSION

While endowed with the ability to autonomously exhibit institutional preferences, and to some extent even advance particular rationales at the expense of others, the European Union cannot escape the fact that it rests on member states.

National political economies exhibit particular configurations of rationales. France has traditionally displayed a strong state power rationale while Germany is characterised by a constitutionally underpinned money market rationale supplemented by a labour market rationale. Finally Britain spouts a dominant pure market rationale occasionally challenged by the state and the labour market sphere.

Regional integration inevitably upsets the national political-economic equilibrium. An exposure of the product market will thus ramify into the labour and money markets. At the same time configurational convergence is a pre-condition for major integrative progress. The pace and direction of regional integrative schemes is thus a product of the ongoing struggle between contending rationales which may expand their respective constituencies from a national to a regional base.

European organisations and institutions have an independent role to play in relation to labour market policy. While conforming to neither states nor market actors such as national social partners, they perform important tasks as policy venues and as bearers, amplifiers and interpreters of ideologies.

Core ingredients of a European level labour market rationale are present in that DGV – headed by a Commissioner – is harbouring formal institutional sanctuary in a political economic setting traditionally predisposed towards product markets. The social partners – the essential posterior of labour market rationales – have apparently replicated the formal organisational structures and institutional mechanisms characteristic of the domestic settings. The question remains whether bearers of this rationale can close ranks and prevail in the EU political economy hosting a fierce struggle between proponents of money market and product market rationales while exhibiting features conducive for state power supremacy.

In the following chapters it will be illustrated how the European level is simultaneously employed by national actors and independently engaged in political struggles sometimes facing other states or European organisations. Hence in chapters 3 and 4 it is examined how three instances of EU labour market policy making has been conducted in an unsettled policy domain lacking both consensus on such a fundamental variable as the need for intervention and coherently organised key actors. As will be demonstrated the social dimension has a history of subjection to different contending rationales severely restricting prospects of long-term institutionalisation.

# 3 Social Protection: Health, Safety and Equal Rights

## 1 INTRODUCTION

This chapter examines two political initiatives in the realm of labour market policy. While formally addressing different issues they both pass under the heading 'social protection'. By contrast chapter 4 probes explicit attempts to erect societal management mechanism by means of the social dialogue.

The first initiative subject to scrutiny falls within the broad category of measures addressing occupational health and safety. The second initiative essentially also concerns work-related safety issues as it deals with the conditions of maternity leave for pregnant woman. However, as pregnancy and child rearing are considered key obstacles for labour market equality between the sexes, the maternity leave directive is commonly assigned to the confinement of the equal opportunity policy arena.

A brief historical review of the evolution of EU labour market policy will introduce the cases. Health, safety and equal opportunity policy form complex legislative bodies featuring key acts constituting legal frameworks. Proceeding from the historical deliberations opening the chapter, both policy fields are gradually narrowed down using the aforementioned key acts as stepping stones. Finally, the passing and substance of the concrete directives are examined. The chapter will conclude with a joint analysis of the two cases in which evidence of colonisation attempts by contending rationales will be identified.

## 2 EU LABOUR MARKET POLICY: AN OVERVIEW

The European Economic Community set up in 1957 was dedicated to the creation of a common market for goods, services, capital and labour. Consequently, the vast majority of initiatives enacted under the heading of 'social policy' is what most North Europeans would brand labour market policy.[77] EU labour market law may be approached both as an integral component of Union legislation, usually aimed at improving internal market operations for goods and labour, and as a distinct field of regulation. A number of directives primarily concerning technical harmonisation may thus contain substantial elements of health and safety regulation while initiatives like the equal pay directive represent law adopted purely for the purpose of labour market regulation.

A committee of experts appointed by the European Coal and Steel Community (ECSC) in cooperation with the International Labour Organisation (ILO) in the fifties concluded that comprehensive Community social and labour market policies were not needed in order to achieve economic integration.[78] Accordingly, the issue remained a marginal area of cooperation – in the sense of a distinct policy field – until later stages of the Union's development.

It is commonplace to divide the development of EU labour market policy into four periods. The first covers the years from the founding of the Communities in 1957 to 1972. This period was concerned with labour market policy to the extent it affected the common market for labour. The second period runs from 1972 to 1980. This period was rather progressive and the scope of previous policies was expanded and new areas for Community action was encompassed by an increasingly ambitious CEU. The third period lasting from 1980 to 1985 was one of stagnation. No major progress in the field was made. In 1985 EU labour market policy saw the light of dawn once again.[79]

Labour mobility and health and safety protection of workers were the only fields where substantial initiatives were made in the first period. Health and safety was mainly addressed, however, to the extent it related to the mobility of the products used as input in industrial production processes.

In connection with the 'relaunch' of the late sixties and early seventies, attempts were made to introduce wider social and labour policy questions on to the Union's agenda. The de facto establishment of the European Council at the Hague summit in 1969 thus gave impetus to the creation of the EPC (European Political Cooperation), the Werner plan for an economic and monetary union and the first social action programme.

The upgrading of social and labour market policies were widely perceived as a response to social unrest which had marred most of the member states during 1967–71. Giving the Community a human face was one of the more cynical ways of describing it. The programme quickly sparked off a reaction in the political environment. As it had been the case in the late fifties where pan-European business-interest associations were formed as a response to the customs union, labour finally got its act together and formed the European Trade Union Confederation out of the traditional antagonist Christian and Socialist associations.

Besides the issues of labour mobility and a markedly upgraded commitment to health and safety, new joint initiatives were announced on labour training and skill acquisition, the rights to organise and undertake industrial actions, and finally the protection of wage earners against excessive exploitation and manipulation in connection with collective dismissals and company closure. These issues were in addition accompanied with policies attempting to introduce minimum rights with regard to information – and occasionally consultation – on management.

Eventually progress came to a halt as consensus on the EU's role in labour and social policy faltered. The latter part of the seventies and the first half of the eighties were characterised by deep divisions between Britain and the other member states.

The successful adoption of the Single European Market scheme (hereafter SEM) was accompanied by renewed calls for a social dimension to the integrative venture. Traditional issues were relaunched and a few new topics were added as the sphere of labour politics had evolved accommodating new problems sparked off by changes in production technology and popular attitudes.

## 2.1 The Social Dimension

Formally launched by the French government the social dimension has been strongly supported by key actors in the CEU since the mid-eighties. It consists of four components:

- A Charter of Fundamental Social Rights of Workers
- A law-catalogue denoted 'The Social Action Programme' aiming at turning parts of the aforementioned Charter into binding legislation
- A European level Social Dialogue between Employers and Employees
- Changing and expanding the Regional-Structural Funds.

Most of the advanced proposals under the Charter and the associated action programme can be traced back to previous attempts of introducing social and labour market regulation at the EU level in the past two decades. Social dialogue similarly has been sought established at previous occasions. Changes to the Regional-Structural Funds are another EU old-timer but will not be considered in this study as the set of issues relating to this field represent an entirely different ball game with emphasis on strictly intergovernmental bargains. Social dialogue is the subject of the next chapter, hence only the remaining two elements of the social dimension will be considered briefly in turn.

## 2.2 The Social Charter

The Community Charter of Fundamental Social Rights of Workers adopted by 11 of the 12 member states at the Strasbourg summit in 1989, was to provide the EU with a basic moral commitment to social progress lacking in the establishing treaties. The fact that it has no binding effect in itself, seriously constrains its ability to ensure progress in the field. But as it was passed as a solemn declaration between the heads of states and governments, its main function was to alter the basic priorities of the Union embedded in the treaties.

The Treaty of Rome had among its general aims to ensure a rising standard of living, but very few commitments were made regarding social distribution and protection. Concrete treaty obligations covering the free movement of labour and establishing a social fund were made. Title III of the treaty was devoted to social policy but has only managed to give impetus to one major area of EU social regulation: equal pay.

In the seventies the lacunae article 235 was cunningly employed by the CEU, but the latter was constrained by its limited applicability as it was confined to areas where full Council consensus existed. In the realm of EU labour market and social policy such areas could be counted on one hand! With the adoption of the Single European Act, an improved constitutional base was provided for the one area not covered by previous treaty commitments but nonetheless subject to some degree of consensus; namely health and safety.

While the Charter is not a treaty amendment but rather the strongest possible signal a split summit could produce, it proved somewhat durable as it was swiftly followed by a Social Action Programme.

**2.3    The Social Action Programme**

The Social Action Programme (SAP) consists of 47 concrete proposals on how to incorporate the principles of the Charter into EU law.
Less than half the proposals are, however, of a binding nature. As
such the SAP builds on the existing tradition of EU legal regulation
of the labour market sphere – relying heavily on soft law – and it is
indeed subject to the same constraints as has been traditionally
conferred upon policy making in the area. EU regulation in the field
of labour market policy can be divided into five headings.

* free movement of persons
* equal treatment of men and women
* the protection of employers' rights in connection with the restructuring of Companies
* information, consultation and worker participation
* the working environment.

Seven more headings are found in both the Charter and the SAP
relating to social policy fields not associated to the labour market.
Only soft law instruments are proposed to be enacted in these
'genuine' social policy areas. The two subject areas singled out for
scrutiny in this study – health and safety and equal treatment – are
separate entries thus signifying their overall importance in the EU's
labour market policy package.

## 3    THE HISTORY OF EU HEALTH AND SAFETY POLICY

Health and safety has been subject to political attention since the
inception of the Union. Particularly so in the Euratom Treaty which
obliged the Union to lay down basic standards regarding exposure of
workers to radiation.[80] Preceding Euratom, the ECSC had taken
initiatives on safety matters in the wake of the 1956 fire catastrophe
at the Bois de Cazier mine (Marcinelle, Belgium) killing 264 workers.
A permanent Mines Safety Commission was established in 1957
bringing together representatives of workers, employers and the then
High Authority.

In 1965 its competence was extended to include health protection
and since 1974 all extractive industries have been encompassed. In
addition the extension of scope prompted a change of name to the

Safety and Health Commission for the Mining and Other Extractive Industries (SHCMOEI).[81] Both ECSC and Euratom have, moreover, conducted important research on the issue of health and safety relating to industrial activities under their purview. However the industries covered by these two treaties are widely considered to be special cases, exactly because of the risks to which they expose their labourers. What concerns us here is occupational health and safety in a rather more broad context. In the sections to come the handling of this matter within the much broader Treaty of Rome will be outlined for each of the four development phases stipulated above.

### The Liberal Phase (1957–72)

In the EEC treaty only the section on transport contained elements conferring competence to formal Union organisations in the field.[82] A Health and Safety division – forerunner of the present Health and Safety Directorate under DGV – was set up by the EEC Commission in 1962. But no joint committee on the subject was created during the first phase of the EU labour market integration process.

Three directives were, nonetheless, proposed between 1964–65, but only one – dealing with classification, labelling and packaging – was adopted in 1967. Although a series of recommendations was approved by the Council in the same period,[83] the directive on classification, labelling and packaging of dangerous substances was by far the most important component of contemporary European level health and safety policy. It effectively established a common market for intermediate goods used in the manufacturing of higher value-added end-products. Hence it supplemented the opening of markets for consumer durables and – to a lesser extent – capital goods.[84]

Consequently the regulation concerned goods rather than people. While the need to protect the plight of workers was implicitly recognised, European level initiatives were aimed at catering to the needs of products markets in alleviating the distortive effects of necessary constraints on the conduct of enterprise. The manner in which this regulation was adopted resembled the workings of the liberal state, fine-tuning the regulatory frameworks of essentially free markets. Accordingly there are little reports of joint committees being erected, upgraded or, for that matter, consulted on the issue. Obviously the ESC was requested to file an opinion and the EEC Commission has surely approached certain affected interests. But unlike contemporary EU labour market politicking there is no evidence of the partnership rhetoric as notoriously aired by present day DGV.

*The Interventionist Phase (1972–80)*
With the 1974 surge in labour market policy the Advisory Committee
on Safety, Hygiene and Health Protection at Work was set up.
Although formally established by the Council its creation was mainly
championed by the CEU.[85] The Committee has 90 members – two
national representatives from respectively member states, employers
and labour – and is chaired by the Commissioner in charge of labour
market affairs. Its composition reflects the classic neo-corporatist
institutional ideal.

These initiatives followed the rising awareness of health and safety
issues prompted by worldwide concerns succeeding discovery of the
carcinogenic nature of vinyl chloride monomer – a substance widely
used in the plastics industry.[86]

The first health and safety action programme adopted by the
Council in 1978 was followed by a second in 1984. In the course of the
programmes three general directives aimed at improving health and
safety at the work place, and three directives dealing with individual
chemical agents, were passed. Of the three general directives the first
and the second concerned safety signs and the general hazards of
exposure to chemical, physical and biological agents respectively. The
third related to the aforementioned issue of applying vinyl chloride
monomer. The more specific directives covered lead, asbestos and
noise.[87] In sum, the issues addressed during this phase were emphasising the technicalities of health and safety policy. The period was
nonetheless characterised by a highly politicised mode of interaction
between the two sides of industry. Given the attention devoted to the
field, it could be expected that more legislation had emerged from the
period. Yet this was the era of the great industrial conflicts.
Antagonism between the social partners thus ramified into the
European level. Yet although progress was mediocre, the second
period brought EU labour market policy out of the realm of pure
market integration. Labour and social policy on a Union level became
an end in itself. A labour market rationale gradually took hold of the
setting leading to the confrontations and stagnation of the subsequent
era.

*Stagnation (1980–86)*
Publicly aired motives for upgrading EU labour market policy in the
seventies rested on 'positive' economic arguments. Often long-term
changes in the world economy were enrolled as arguments support-
ing this development. The rise of the multinationals and growing

internationalisation of production thus prompted calls for regulatory structures replacing the increasingly powerless nation states.

Increasing the geographical mobility of European labour and meeting the expected challenge of the internationalisation of production, could assumably be accommodated better on a European level. Harmonisation was thus regarded as a means of establishing transparency. Labour was expected to be more inclined to move between member states if no risks existed for losing benefit rights earned in one country due to incompatibilities in social legislation. International capital could also benefit from transparency since, for example, making 'the international car' would require less corporate planning if, say, work time rules were unanimous throughout the region. Only one set of legal codes and collective agreements would thus assist the region in adapting to the changes in the functioning of the international economy. In contrast to this line of reasoning, business, typically nationally rooted in only one of the member states, argued against labour market harmonisation as uniform provisions were seen to cause inflexibility due to differences in the production conditions in the member countries.

In spite of vigorous labour support, but perhaps because of similarly vigorous resistance from business, the first social action programme produced only two major results: a comprehensive and generally recognised policy for promoting the rights of women in the economic sphere and a number of directives providing workers with minimum protection in relation to mass dismissals, transfer of undertakings and mergers. Minor policy initiatives regarding the integration of physically disabled people were also adopted but regardless of the sympathetic gesture of this move, it was of limited impact on the overall industrial relations questions.

The infamous Fifth Draft Directive as well as the Vredeling Directive proposal for labour co-determination in major European corporations, were effectively defeated bringing the whole process to a standstill. Yet the relative organisational strength of labour versus business interests, cannot in itself explain the limited results of the action programme. International crisis and de-industrialisation of the late sixties and early seventies brought about an urge to adopt national solutions to replace eroding international management regimes.[88] This aggravated the labour market integration process as national governments on the continent increasingly came to see labour relations as a strategic factor in strengthening national competition and product innovation and, as differences in national institutional capabilities varied tremendously, saw little reason to risk this vital policy instrument in a diffuse and inadequately organised European arena.[89]

Both the second and the third phase was subject to colonisation efforts from the labour market rationale. Legislation increasingly concerned workers instead of products. Confrontation dominated the policy process and prevalent rhetoric described the stakes in zero-sum terms as 'opponents' were 'forced' to 'concede'. Policy-making bodies reflecting neo-corporatist designs were erected and the policy agenda was considerably expanded.

All possible labour concerns thus seemed to require European level action. As the Werner plan took shape it was widely considered natural that the broader political economic structures of the welfare state were elevated to the European level. This obviously complicated the process.

Both the Werner plan and the tacit ambition to erect a European level welfare regime re-opened national struggles on basic political economic strategies. National welfare state designs reflected different equilibriums between contending rationales. As the European level political system geared itself towards addressing these issues it faced deadlock as no convergence in preferences were evident among constituent units. During the interventionist phase a number of grand style venues were erected. As it will be discussed in chapter 4 their composition and function resembled the macro-institutional matrix of classical neo-corporatism. High profiled antagonism was vividly displayed in these settings effectively overshadowing other venues increasingly stalemated by deadlock at the peak-level. Eventually policy contradictions on almost every issue led to a clean brake as labour walked out of certain strategic settings thus prompting intervention to give way to the stagnant phase.

*The Participatory Phase (1986–)*
Establishing common technical standards for capital goods is a cornerstone of the internal market. The thrust for technical harmonisation reached far into the realm of working environment regulation.

The Single European Act introduced article 118A firmly establishing health and safety as a Union policy field. It in addition allowed for use of qualified majority voting in relation to health and safety legislation. Following the ratification of SEA in 1987 a third, highly ambitious, action programme was adopted by the Council. A number of directives on health and safety were proposed – and some even adopted – under the auspices of the social charter and its accompanying action programme making this area subject to more extensive EU regulation than any other field within the realm of labour market policy.[90]

Following the successful abolition of most tariff related trade barriers by the late sixties, a number of member states introduced numerous NTBs in the wake of the first oil crisis. Although NTBs had been in operation several years prior to the recession, their growing numbers and increasingly bold discriminatory nature ensured them a prominent position on Council minutes.

Countering protectionistic trends was obviously recognised as a task for the Union. The CEU sought to achieve harmonisation of national standards by proposing directives containing exhaustive technical specifications. These very detailed and comprehensive directive proposals, were to be adopted unanimously by the Council. This route proved very troublesome, and the success rate of CEU proposals in the Council was very modest indeed. Consequently, a new approach to this category of regulation was devised.

The new approach embodied a purge of detailed technical specifications from directive proposals, leaving only overall guidelines to be adopted by the Council. More specific standards were consequently left to be worked out by the association of national standardisation bodies, which in turn invited all affected groupings – willing to sponsor standardisation work – to participate.[91] Council decisions were thus to constitute legal frameworks to be filled out by the affected parties – a mode of private government increasingly practised in national systems.

The secretariats of CEN and CENELEC were approached by the Commission in 1984 as the latter was planning to introduce the new approach according the two standardisation bodies a prominent role in the working out of detailed technical specifications. As a response to the reform, new working procedures for CEN and CENELEC were made. These were designed in a manner ensuring a high degree of compatibility between the working and structure of the two organisations. These changes did produce some tensions as national bodies had been engaged in mutual rivalry on several occasions but the CEU managed to persuade all parties as it held out two irresistible carrots: the funding and the lucrative prospects of a genuine internal market.[92]

Participation in, and funding of, national standardisation work varies considerably between countries. Participating interests are usually drawn from producers, research communities, regulatory agencies, consumers, professional societies and – in some countries – trade unions. Representatives from affected interests constitute technical committees working under the auspices of a branch committee. National committees send delegates to the CEN/CENELEC corresponding committee where agreements and understandings concluded at the national level are bended towards a common position.[93] Besides nationally appointed representatives, EU wide interests have a voice in the works of CEN/CENELEC as European associations can participate although they have no vote.

It has been the express intention of the new approach to relate the health and safety provisions with the free movement of (capital) goods.[94] As venues of labour market policy making, CEN/CENELEC pose a severe challenge to the labour market rationale. Voluntary participation conditional only upon financial contribution, paired with a mode of operation stressing research based and strictly economically founded technical arguments, clearly diverge from the power-based tradition highlighting social collective constituencies dominant in the previous phase. Unlike venues designed in accordance with the labour market rationale, standardisation committees cherish a technocratic cooperative culture incompatible with, for example, threats of extra-committee action such as strikes.

While committee voting may be employed, procedures are not really democratic as votes are not weighted according to the size of constituencies. Market power, on the other hand, does not sum up the operational mode of the committees either. Although there is a premium on participation, big firms are not necessarily in a favourable position vis-à-vis smaller firms or dedicated research organisations. Evidently a high intelligence and research capacity is conducive for the success with which committee participants advance their views. Yet size may still be countered by specialised skills.

CEN/CENELEC falls between the market-hierarchy dichotomy in that they ascribe to a network mode of operation. Hence a plurality of actors, submitting to no particular peak-setting, pit their technical skills against one another in an effort to arrive at broadly accepted solutions legitimised by their superior qualities. Clearly the single market signalled a new phase in EU labour market regulation going beyond both the state power, the product market and the labour market rationales.

Impetus for reviving EU labour market policy thus largely stems from health and safety issues arising out of SEM. Particularly one directive provided the linkage between internal market aspirations and labour market policy rejuvenation.

### 3.1 The Adoption of the Machinery Directive

The Machinery Directive, originally adopted by the Council in late 1989, sets out to regulate 'the most important requirements regarding security and health conditions in connection with machine operation, stability, bodily hazards, shielding, and danger of fire, explosion, and radiation, as well as noise, vibration, emission of particles and gases etc. and hygienic precautions'. Aimed at manufacturers of machinery the directive spells out a number of standards industrial machines will have to conform to in order to be marketable in the EU.

Article 100A of the SEA stipulates that directives concerning technical harmonisation are to be adopted on a qualified majority basis. The Machinery Directive is by far the most comprehensive of the directives adopted under this article and in addition constitutes a core element of the internal market scheme. According to CEU estimates the aggregated revenue of the engineering industry amounted to approximately 200 billion ECU in 1989. Roughly 10 per cent of the business is subject to regulation by the directive.[95] The Machinery Directive was to come into effect by December 1992, but was postponed until late 1994 due to delays both at the Council and the CEN/CENELEC level. Some six months after its initial decision to pass the act, the Council was thus confronted by a number of major revisions from the CEU. They mainly consisted of specific guidelines for machinery not covered by the original proposal.

Although the directive was proposed in extension of the SEM – and thus not subject to labour market policy consultation procedures – the CEU contacted the European Committee of Construction Equipment Producers (CECE), European Manufacturers of Agriculture Machinery (CEMA), European Transport Material Producer Association (FEM), ETUC and representatives of the member states.[96] In addition representatives of CEN/CENELEC were consulted at this early phase together with SHCMOEI and the Advisory Committee on Safety, Hygiene and Health Protection at Work. The latter established an ad hoc committee which sent a delegation to the CEU expert committee working on the proposal.[97] The access points of affected interest – not directly approached – were in addition substantial due to the CEU's practice of consulting a vast range of advisory groups including the ESC.

All consulted interests and bodies came out in favour of the directive and its delay can be attributed to two factors: first, the CEU had initially decided not to cover 'mobile' equipment by the directive. Consequently, the original proposal put forward to the Council in 1987 and adopted on 14 June 1989, was replaced by a revised proposal of 15 December 1989 including 'mobile' equipment. Secondly, the directive resulted in a large number of standards having to be worked out – a time consuming enterprise even with the new procedure.

Initial consultations on the directive were of a highly technical nature. Employers soon proved to possess a much higher level of professional expertise than trade unions. As trade unions in addition were represented solely by their peak organisation, ETUC, in committees consulted by the CEU at the initial stage of the process, the impact of labour was greatly impaired due to both technical and numerical inferiority. Consequently ETUC decided to upgrade its competence in the field by establishing the 'European Trade Union Technical Bureau for Health and Safety (TUTB).' This decision was taken in close cooperation with CEU which offered to sponsor most TUTB activities.[98]

The CEU pursued a line of highly selective direct consultation thus putting employers, or rather business associations, at an advantage. On the side of employers, several intermediate associations were involved at the preparatory stage together with the peak association whereas only ETUC, on the side of labour was directly consulted. This reflects the fact that the managing Directorate General was DGIII – industrial affairs – rather than the labour market oriented DGV.

The decision to fund safety and health research – or more correctly, competence upgrading – at ETUC, was taken by DGV. While labour was manifestly weak at the preparatory stage of the policy process they have, with active consent of the CEU, participated much more strongly in the standardisation work carried out under the auspices of CEN/CENELEC.[99]

The Machinery Directive was to be the first challenge for national industrial relation systems stemming from the internal market scheme, which at this point enjoyed the general backing of trade unions and employer associations alike. In addition the directive served as an eye-opener for European level bearers of the labour market rationale. Yet little in the way of societal pressures from the social partners materialised.[100] Rather, other branches of the CEU intervened to upgrade labour. The newly gained goodwill of the

CEU enabled it to pursue cautious labour market policy without immediately being slated by wary Council members. As the President had expressed a key interest in the field, DGV stepped in as an active player in the shaping of a labour market component to the internal market scheme. The CEU independently mobilised the trade union movement thus demonstrating its relative autonomy of member states which – with the notable exception of France – at this stage expressed little interest in balancing the product market rationale of the internal market scheme with a labour component.

This mobilisation process was thus to become instrumental for the adoption of a separate Framework Directive, regulating the interaction of workers and capital equipment, conforming to the common standards spelled out in the Machinery Directive.

### 3.2 The Adoption of the Framework Directive

Directive 89/391/EEC introducing measures to encourage improvements in the safety and health of workers, lays down minimum requirements in the field which member states were under no circumstances to fail to satisfy by 31 December 1992. Although widely attributed to the Social Charter the directive was in fact proposed in connection with the action programme on health and safety of 1987 – two years before the commitment to a social dimension was made by member states. While health and safety make up the most extensive section of the social action programme, it lists neither the Framework Directive nor any of the accompanying individual directives.[101] The Framework Directive was adopted according to article 118A of the SEA which allows for qualified majority. It nonetheless passed unanimously in the Council in spite of a comprehensive section on worker participation in the handling of health and safety issues at the firm level – a point usually prompting British resistance.[102]

Article 16 of the directive specifies a number of individual directives to be adopted within the framework of 89/391/EEC coping with particular risks. The Framework Directive thus does not contain a technical section but rather general guidelines stipulating the obligations of employers and workers, the principle of substitution – that is, replacing dangerous agents with less dangerous ones where possible – and procedures for information, consultation and participation of workers.[103] Nine individual directives, making explicit reference to the general philosophy and procedures stipulated in the Framework Directive, have been adopted.[104]

Whereas the Machinery Directive is absolute in the standards set out – that is, they cannot be derogated on the grounds of national health and safety concerns – the Framework Directive is a minimum directive allowing – even calling – for extensive national derogations on the basis of national health and safety regulation.[105]

Instituting legislative bodies by means of Framework Directives in EU health and safety, has precedence in directive 80/1107/EEC on the protection of workers from risks related to exposure to chemical, physical and biological agents at work. Like directive 89/391/EEC it calls for the adoption of individual directives, regulating in more detail the handling of particular agents. Unlike the 1989 directive, 80/1107/EEC does not contain an elaborate section on the participation of workers in health and safety issues nor does it place particular obligations on employers but rather calls for member states to ensure compliance with the principles stipulated.

Some practicians of labour law consider the 1989 Framework Directive an improvement vis-à-vis national standards.[106] But given the nature of the directive the positive effects mainly relate to the issues of employer responsibility and participation of workers.

Arguably the Framework Directive is essentially aimed at establishing a European industrial relation system on occupational health.[107] Hence individual directives have only raised national levels of equivalent health and safety standards to a limited extent. Accordingly, for example, the sixth directive under 89/392 on exposure to carcinogens, only tightens the substitution principle already spelled out in the Framework Directive. The technical value limits, annexed to the directive, represents no major advance compared to existing EU legislation in the field. The provisions on participation in the Framework Directive – which in addition are mentioned directly in individual directives – are by contrast novel and constitute a challenge to existing practices of certain EU members.

In article 1 the objective of the Framework Directive is stated. Already at this stage a substantial part of the text is devoted to the question of participation. Articles 10, 11 and, to some extent, 12 deal with worker information, the training of workers or their representatives and guidelines for general participation. Article 11 in particular dwells on participation. Employers shall thus:

[C]onsult workers and/or their representatives and allow them to take part in discussion on all questions relating to safety and health at work.[108]

The directive explicitly presupposes that workers are consulted, that they are allowed to make proposals and that some system of *balanced* participation is established according to national laws and/or practices. Worker representatives shall be allowed time off, without loss of pay, and granted the necessary means to exercise their rights and functions, in addition they shall be entitled to appeal to competent authorities if they consider measures taken in the health and safety field inappropriate. Finally, workers or worker representatives may not be placed at a disadvantage because of their activities referred to in the directive.[109] In sum, provisions on labour participation overshadow advances in terms of value limits and other technicalities.

When looking at the policy process, the adoption of the Framework Directive signalled a re-configuration of the setting. Hence the Advisory Committee on Safety, Hygiene and Health Protection was upgraded – by the CEU![110] This body signals a return to traditional tri-partism as associated with the labour market rationale. Yet the committee incorporated some of the technocratic currents evident in the CEN/CENELEC setting. In addition it relied on the CEU for sponsorship and its new won feathers as a high-grade dialogue venue. More importantly, however, the committee was in a state of constant competition with the very dynamic arenas handling technical harmonisation. Decisions in the realm of CEN/CENELEC thus effectively framed options and set the pace. This caused some self-restraint prompting committee members to approach the issues in a rather more cooperative manner. Anatagonism was thus partly deflected from internal deliberation towards competing decision-making centres. As a policy health and safety was perceived as a battleground – not between Council members or the social partners – but rather the market crusaders of DGIII and its client settings, and the not entirely legitimate social backdrop performed by DGV and friends.

Immediately after its establishment the committee had asked the CEU to inform it well in advance of initiatives on health and safety. It appears that cooperation between the committee and the CEU evolved smoothly although the level of activity slowly declined from 1979 to 1985. When learning of the CEU's work on establishing an internal market, the committee deplored the fact it had not been consulted on issues of technical harmonisation and health and safety. In addition labour representatives expressed some reservations with regard to the new approach to technical harmonisation as it had been worked out by CEU and CEN/CENELEC. Although the committee came out in favour of the new approach, DGV – and the President's cabinet – seized the opportunity to propagate the image of social partners' discontent with the procedural handling of the internal market programme. Concerns for the social balance of the liberalisation process were aired and essentially this was to be the occasion for letting DGV into the mainstreams of project 1992 – although the presidency had a keen eye to the activities of the Directorate General and its Commissioner.[111]

Consequently the CEU involved the committee actively in the drawing up of its third action programme on health and safety. Participants were given privileged access to the critical drafting stage. In the action programme social dialogue became an area of high priority. The CEU used the occasion to stress the role of the committee as a forum of social dialogue. In addition the Council resolution enacting the social action programme contained two explicit references to the committee in the final text. Hence both governments, employer and trade union representatives emphasised the venue's function as a dialogue setting, and it soon experienced a surge in the level of activity.[112]

As a European level dialogue venue, the committee differs from the Val Duchesse setting in that it is composed of national representatives rather than delegates of the European level social partners. However, both employer and labour committee members come from affiliates of ETUC and UNICE. In addition the secretariats and organisational structures of the European associations increasingly assume an important role in coordinating views etc. The very growth in committee activities has prompted a need for stronger coordination, thus from 1985 to 1989 the amount of annual meetings went up from 9 to 47 and the number of days spent in session grew from 16 to 70.[113] Growing needs for coordination stemming from increased importance and rising level of activities prompted labour to appoint a representative of ETUC as spokesperson.[114] Finally, the fact that states are directly represented is considered a strength as the committee is to serve as an input to the traditional EU policy-making process which places the Council in a central position. The Val Duchesse setting by contrast is intended as an entirely new setting of policy making bypassing states.[115]

Consultation on the Framework Directive between the CEU and the committee peaked in the winter of 1987/88 where a long series of meetings were held in Luxembourg.[116] Meanwhile in the Council, prospects of having the directive adopted on a qualified majority basis turned Britain into a surprisingly constructive player. The UK decided to accept the sections on worker participation. From the perspective of London the battle had apparently been lost with the inclusion of article 118A in the SEA, and rather than suffering a series of predictable and humiliating defeats in health and safety, the Conservative government under John Major deemed it more fruitful to combat the Social Dimension elsewhere.[117] The humiliation of having to accept EU legislation stipulating the rights of workers to intrude on traditional management prerogatives, was smoothened by German, Dutch and Danish attempts to moderate the progressive wording of the proposed directive.[118] As conflict concerned participation rather than health and safety provisions, eight of the individual directives passed through the Council in a relatively smooth fashion.

In sum, Council deliberations conformed to the supranational ideals as defined by Haas (1964b). Partnership prevailed over antagonism. As Council proponents of the directive closed ranks, Britain gave in. Humiliation was, however, avoided as core supporters of the Framework Directive, embarked on a policy of compromise once a qualified majority had been assured.

By contrast it was the stated intention of the majority labour market policy coalition in the European Parliament to use this type of legislation to introduce a EU-wide system of information and consultation rights.[119]

Traditionally taking on the role as progressive cadres of European labour market policy, the European Parliament played an important role as the Framework Directive was adopted according to the procedures spelled out in article 149 of the SEA. The cooperation procedure thus obliges the CEU and the Council to submit directive proposals for a second reading in the EP. At the second reading the Parliament may, acting on absolute majority, force the Council to resort to unanimous voting should they wish to adopt a proposal against the will of the EP. This option is applicable only in a limited number of the policy fields allowing for qualified majority Council voting.

Widespread discontent existed in the EP over what was considered as a narrow interpretation of health and safety. According to MEPs the Framework Directive was too restrictive in its application as it was confined to health and safety at the workplace. The CEU pledges that ergonomics would be addressed in an individual directive persuaded the Socialist-Christian Democratic alliance, thus ensuring the proposal a fairly smooth passage through the readings. Of additional importance was the extensive section on participation included in the draft and eventually – to everybody's surprise – the final version.[120]

The ESC also endorsed the Framework Directive and the first individual directives accompanying it.[121] While the majority for approval was overwhelming, it was granted on the grounds that the directives was a promising albeit not entirely satisfactory beginning of EU occupational health and safety legislation.

The surprisingly easy passage of the Framework Directive through both the Advisory Committee, the Council, the EP and the ESC signals first the non-contagious nature of the technical standards set and secondly the broad consensus regarding the desirability of promoting interaction between management and labour in a flexible manner at the firm level. As standards defined in the accompanying individual directives would only effect minor adjustments in member states, there were no economic costs involved for economically less advanced members in adopting them. As they were merely minimum standards there were no political costs for the more advanced countries in subscribing to them.

What the directive did ensure was a uniform set of guidelines providing some form of worker participation at the firm level. These guidelines are designed in a rather flexible manner which conforms to existing systems in most of the continental member states. Continental members who were only beginning to establish industrial relation sub-systems for health and safety, were blessed with a general political consensus on the importance of upgrading this aspect of labour regulation. Britain, which has an elaborate industrial relations sub-system for dealing with health and safety, abandoned her resistance to legal codification of labour rights in this domain. Hence the Major government decided not to invest political resources and prestige on a battle which could not be won.

Little has been achieved in terms of improving – even harmonising – health and safety standards, beyond what is embodied in the design of the machinery and substances used in the production process, however, the policy process leading up to the adoption of both the Machinery Directive, the Framework Directive and the actual contents of the latter has served to intensify political action of the social partners at the EU level and even harmonise the nature of interaction between management and labour on the national level.

### 3.3 Health and Safety Strategies: From Transactional Efficiency to Trust Enhancement

Historically, EU health and safety policy is linked to product rather than labour market operations. Establishing a regulatory regime ensuring free flows of goods was the justification for embarking on the common market venture in the first place.

Labour market policy was marginalised in the first treaties. Old fashion neo-functionalist spillover assured a comeback in that health and safety measures became intrinsic for the success of the SEM. While initial initiatives in the field adhered more to concerns for businesses than workers, they gradually paved the way for consensus on the growing need for broad EU competence in the field.

The internal market scheme – hallmark of the product market rationale – was instrumental in upgrading European level labour market policy. By thoroughly colonising the area a product market logic had prevailed in Union labour market policy design. However the enhancement of scope and procedural improvements admitted through product market needs, constituted a basis for charges from contending rationales.

Participation thus springs out of a rationale negating the pure market ideal as a foundation for social organisation. Assessed on the wording of the aforementioned directive it appears to subscribe to key virtues of the labour market rationale. Participation is thus to be 'balanced' and the integrity of worker representatives is specifically addressed. Yet, firm level antagonism in the conduct of industrial relations is taken into account, hence partnership and similar jargon associated to catholic social teachings, for example, permeate the text.

In the Machinery Directive a number of interests were consulted individually while most of the interaction with interest groupings in connection with the Framework Directive was confined to the Advisory Committee. The CEU thus sought to create a fixed pattern of interaction and in the process gave privileged access to peak representatives seated in the committee. In return labour made particular efforts to achieve supranational coherence between national trade union representatives by upgrading the role of ETUC in the coordination work.

Passing the Framework Directive was an exercise in social dialogue in itself. Perhaps more importantly the impact of the directive is mainly going to be enhancing a similar process at the firm level. The firm level provisions for participation may erode the virtues of neo-corporatist intermediation as associated with the previous reign of the labour market rationale. The sort of venues created at firm level do not owe their existence to previous show-downs between successful trade unions and conceding employer associations. Rather they are imposed by law and operate only with firm level workers and management rather than union representatives. The jargon employed suggests that they are to conform to an operational ideal more aligned to the network based mode of interaction than traditional power based antagonism. What matters seems to be ensuring a pattern of labour-management interaction not inviting excessive confrontation. To this end health and safety provides a consensus-ridden policy field featuring technical problems to be solved mainly at the shop-floor. In sum, the focus of EU health and safety has been diverted from a product market orientation, towards a somewhat fluid institutional state, combining elements of traditional labour market virtues with networking and trust enhancing mechanisms aligned to the money market rationale.

In the next case we will probe into EU equal opportunities policy. The EU's record in this field is fairly impressive but cannot unambiguously be traced back to narrow economic concerns. As shall be demonstrated it nonetheless received additional momentum following advances in health and safety.

## 4   THE HISTORY OF EQUAL OPPORTUNITY IN THE EU

When assessing the success of EU labour market policy since the enactment of the 1958 EEC Treaty, three areas stand out. The first and second are policies associated to the free movement of labour and health and safety. Both these policies were, however, adopted to enable the free movement of production factor inputs, for example, labour and chemical substances. The third issue area, equal opportunity, can therefore be regarded as the most elaborate and successful genuine EU labour market policy. Yet its inclusion in the EU legal body was nonetheless initially justified by means of purely economic arguments.

During early negotiations on the setting up of the EEC, in particular French negotiators emphasised the need for labour market policy measures. As mentioned in section 2, German and Benelux negotiators managed to fend off French attempts of inserting extensive labour market provisions in the Treaty of Rome by pointing to the recently published Ohlin Report written under the auspices of ILO in 1956.[122]

French woes about the potential distortive effects of their relatively expensive social schemes mainly funded by employer contributions, were appeased by the Ohlin report arguing that the mode of financing national social programmes was irrelevant to the operation of a common market. To some extent French concerns were based on genuine labour cost-differences faced by the country's producers in comparison to industry of the other founding members. French labour legislation contained provisions nominally ensuring equal pay between men and women thus posing the segments of French manu-facturing industry employing many female workers (e.g. textile) with a competitive disadvantage.

French concerns with equal pay are commonly attributed to the country's massive losses of manpower in two world wars – periodically making the influx of women to the labour force a precondition for sustained production levels – and the legacy of citizenship in political and legal philosophy informing French state elites. Citizenship and equal treatment are linked by intellectual bonds most manifestly displayed by liberal state conceptions, departing from inherent rights conferred upon individuals at the time of birth. While advocates of liberal state theory have advanced imaginative intellectual constructs with a view to evade the inevitable elevation of women to full citizen-ship, the liberal state also constituted the base for universal suffrage propagated on the grounds of human rights and Christianity. French insistence on including article 119 in the Treaty of Rome – stipulating the principle of equal pay – is rooted in structural traits of that country's labour market, moulded by institutionally underpinned ideals on equality exhibited by the liberal state power rationale.

This article was later to constitute a cornerstone in the CEU's pursuit of a European labour market policy and has in addition provoked a long series of European Court of Justice (ECJ) cases, the most important conferred by Belgian courts. Acting on behalf of Ms Defrenne, a Sabena air hostess, feminist lawyer Eliane Vogel-Polsky accused the Belgian national airline of offering dissimilar and discriminating terms of employment for stewards and stewardesses. Belgian courts referred a series of questions to the ECJ which even-tually ruled in favour of direct enforceability of article 119. Institutionally the ECJ harbours ideals on power and governance intrinsic to national state apparatuses. This is not to imply that the ECJ acts in accordance with the wishes or interests of states. Rather it extends the logic of state power to the European level. Submission to legal authority by all societal actors is an essential component of the liberal state. Hence initial advances in EU equal opportunity were carried forth by actors adhering to the state sphere.

By 1 January 1982 an Advisory Committee on Equal Opportunity for Women and Men was established. CEU appointed committees usually consist of members allotted on a European rather than a national basis. However, in this case members are appointed from official national bodies dealing with equal opportunity issues. The European social partners may attend meetings as observers according to procedures determined by the Advisory Committee and the CEU. Two members are appointed from each national body – in case more than one national body is in operation, the CEU chooses the one appearing most representative and independent.[123] There have been attempts from the side of ETUC to make the committee a genuinely tripartite setting.[124] In effect the constitution of the committee has been disputed as ideals on institutional design, oscillating between network and power bargaining, have been attempted to be imposed on the venue. Hence equal opportunity councils do not pit men and women representatives against one another *per se*. Rather they offer cooperative settings in which opinions – rather than 'objective interests' – are mended towards 'common understandings'. This network mode of interaction obviously contravenes the institutional foundation of mainstream labour market bodies.

Between 1975 and 1986 five directives were passed with explicit reference to the issue of equal treatment.[125] They have all been advanced in accordance with the original Treaty articles 100 and/or 235, both of which are essentially catch-all articles allowing the EU to adopt policies within areas not covered by more specific provisions. The disadvantage of adhering to article 100 and/or 235 lies in that the Council must rule unanimously in order to adopt legislation.

Three action programmes on equality have been enacted one of which is still running at the time of writing. The first action programme emanated from a conference held in Manchester, England in 1980. It was commenced in 1982 – running from 1982 to 1985 – and contained sixteen specific action areas one of which concerned protecting women during pregnancy and motherhood.[126] A second programme running from 1986 to 1990 was adopted replacing the first programme. While stating that it was continuing with the themes of the first programme, seven – rather more broad – central areas of priority were singled out. These included employment, social security and family responsibilities.

A third programme was adopted by the CEU on 17 October 1990.[127] The first two programmes provided specific measures to be transformed into either binding legislation or soft law. In addition traditional Union initiatives in peripheral policy areas such as information exchange and research were enacted.[128] The third equality programme, however, signalled a change of emphasis. Accordingly equal opportunity issues were increasingly to be incorporated into the EU's economic and structural policies. Concepts such as 'complementarity' and 'subsidiarity' have emerged on the agenda giving prominence to increased direct cooperation between the 'equality partners' at the expense of targeted directives in the field.[129]

Only one of the directives passed in the period 1975–86 contained direct reference to the first action programme. A fourth directive was submitted by the CEU on parental leave. This directive, which also explicitly referred to the first equal treatment programme, was blocked by the Council. Following the adoption of the second programme another three directives were submitted to the Council. The first is dated 27 October 1987 and follows up on the two previous directives on equal treatment in social security adopted in 1979 and 1986 respectively. The second was submitted on 27 May 1988 and concerns the burden of proof in relation to equal treatment. Finally, a proposal for a directive on the protection of pregnant women at the workplace was first forwarded to the Council on 18 September 1990 and later amended on 8 January 1991. While both the first and second directive in this batch are explicitly related to the second action programme this is not the case of the Pregnancy Directive which is attached to the Framework Directive on health and safety.

This marks a shift of CEU strategy which in the first equality programme had announced the proposal as part of the then hitherto most successful EU labour market policy: equal treatment. The proposal re-surfaced in connection with the social charter and the accompanying Social Action Programme (SAP). The following sections will examine how and why this connection was made.

### 4.1 Equal Opportunity, the Charter and the Action Programmes

Political attention to the labour market aspects of European integration experienced a renaissance with newly elected French President François Mitterand's launch of his 'Espace Social Europe' in 1981. The Social Charter of the internal market was first introduced at the executive level by the Belgian Presidency in 1987. But it was only on the European Council meeting in Hanover on 27–28 June 1988 advances were made as the final summit communiqué contained a statement announcing the Council's aspirations to see the internal market conceived in a manner benefiting all citizens of the EU. Direct reference was made to the ambition of improving working conditions, the standard of living and health and safety protection of wage earners.

The CEU was invited to act by putting forward material on how to address the issues. The Commissioner then in charge of labour market affairs, Manuel Marin, in September 1988 published a report on the plans of the CEU concerning the social dimension. The report was, however, generally not considered comprehensive enough by trade unionists and consequently became subject to extensive criticism.

In the meantime CEU president Jacques Delors had addressed the General Assembly of ETUC's 1988 Congress in Stockholm. He once again emphasised that the internal market scheme would benefit wage earners, albeit the full potential of the scheme could be utilised only if the labour movement took part in the shaping of a new Europe.[130]

Mobilisation of labour was further intensified as Delors requested the ESC to draw up a framework for the Social Dimension. A statement, known as the Social Charter, was published in early 1989. The initial Belgian initiative had promulgated:

> [A] sister to the European Convention of Human Rights should be adopted in some revised form by the Community.[131]

ESC delegates from the social partners agreed on the contents of the fundamental labour related and social rights drawing on past conventions of the European Council, OECD and ILO. Ambiguity as to whether or not the ESC envisioned their charter backed up by binding or non-binding regulation, is reflected in a curious statement from the document claiming that

> to lay down rules also means to define a platform of rights below which it is not possible either to bargain or legislate at national level.[132]

Interestingly, consensus prevailed in the ESC – which is mainly composed of representatives from national labour and employer associations – on not having a labour code at the European level as:

Member States and the two sides of industry in these Member States must remain free to legislate and to sign collective agreements.[133]

In reality trade unions and employer associations on the European level were, however, far from being in agreement over the Charter. ETUC advocated a maximalist's approach whereas European employers wanted non-binding principles to which companies and member states could aspire.[134]

Although publicly advocating a maximalist approach, internally the Commissioners discussed whether it was legally and politically feasible to convert the Charter into binding rules, as, apart from health and safety, there was only a limited mandate for such legislation in the Treaty of Rome. The initial CEU decision of refraining from converting the Charter into binding legislation had been the outcome of heated debate among Commissioners. Jacques Delors and Manuel Marin found themselves in minority on the issue as prominent free-marketers in the Commission headed by Lord Cockfield and Henning Christoffersen advocated soft law instruments supplemented with agreements reached via social dialogue.

While Delors preferred a European social regime based on negotiated settlements rather than legislative measures, he needed an instrument to squeeze reluctant employers into an arrangement sufficiently comprehensive to ensure trade union compliance with the Internal Market Scheme. Labour market legislation could be used as a tool for nurturing dialogue.[135]

Discontented with having yet another promising agreement buried in hollow recommendations and good intentions, ETUC, in March 1989, approached the socialist group in the European Parliament and persuaded them to resist further proposals for the internal market scheme unless the CEU put forward binding directive proposals. After the summer 1989 elections where the Socialists, Communists and Greens achieved a majority, the former repeated their commitment to ETUC. The CEU gave in to the pressure and agreed with labour ministers of the member states on a plan according to which ESC's Social Charter was to be rewritten as a Union-pact on basic social and labour market related rights. The pact was in turn to be translated into directive proposals by the CEU.[136]

In May 1989, the CEU produced a draft text of the Social Charter and at the Madrid summit in June 1989 a consensus seemed to emerge among member states. Soon after the summit, however,

Britain raised doubts as to the purpose and form – if any – of EU labour market policy. This prompted the French Presidency, which had taken a strong interest in the matter, to speed up processing of the Charter.

The Socialist French administration considered itself as vanguard of the Charter in light of Mitterand's early statement on the issue. As discussed in chapter 2, France has struggled to profoundly alter its political economy. EU was a vehicle in this attempt. Having experienced high growth rates in the first two decades after the Second World War, the country faced stagnation as the seventies was marked by sluggish growth and chronically fiscal imbalances. The SEM was accepted as a component in the integrative scheme adding economic vitality to both France and neighbouring markets. However, as a model for societal organisation, the pure market ideal implied in the product market rationale of the SEM was strongly rejected by, in particular, the socialist segment of France's political elite. As the country's political economic transformation made it vulnerable to the onslaught of market forces, the state had an incentive to supplement the SEM with policy initiatives embedded in an institutional set-up informed by either the money or labour market rationale.

Yet, when assessing the role of France, the SEM and accelerated European integration should not merely be regarded as external threats prompting state action. France and her major partners agreed on the scheme because there was a convergence in national appreciation of drastic joint European action to counter the malice of Eurosclerosis. Intensified European integration was thus partly to provide the dynamics for domestic change. Implied in socialist reform plans was the aspiration to import institutional features of the social market economy associated with Germany and a number of small north-western European countries. The first years of the Mitterrand administration saw the initiation of ambitious labour market reform and attempts of rejuvenating the country's science and technology system. Public coffers suffered severely from these attempts resulting in the crumbling of the Franc on international currency markets and a humiliating near withdrawal from the recently established Exchange Rate Mechanism (ERM).

As going alone did not produce desired results the French state emerged from the crisis with renewed commitment to a European approach. As change could not be effectuated by domestic measures, the French state demonstrated its capacity for diachronic coherence by enrolling her European partners for the task. As running a ballot in French electoral politics stipulating institutional import from Germany is unlikely to be successful, the 'necessity discourse' was invoked as senior French Socialist Jacques Delors was shipped to Brussels to stir up external pressures for domestic reform.

In close cooperation with the CEU the French Presidency aimed at reaching an agreement by the December 1989 summit as it was not expected that the Irish – who were next in line for the Council chair – could handle the task.[137] The CEU's contribution in speeding up the time schedule was to publish a so-called 'Finalised Draft' of the Charter by September 1989.

At the Strasbourg summit on 8 December 1989, eleven of the twelve heads of state approved the pact as the Social Charter and in January 1990 the CEU submitted an Action Programme for the Charter's implementation and forwarded seven directive proposals.[138] While numerous concessions were made to Britain's Margaret Thatcher, Her Majesty's Government decided not to assent and a tacit accord on disagreement was reached between the UK and the other member states.

On the basis of the Social Charter the social action programme converting the basic rights into EU law was drawn up by the CEU. Of the 47 proposed measures roughly half was intended to have legal effect. The most controversial measures are directive proposals aiming at establishing European-wide minimum standards for the rights and legal protection of workers.

Amid strong criticism in a number of member countries by trade unions and employer associations alike, the CEU initiated a new procedure in the context of the social dialogue during January 1990. The social partners were to be invited as early as possible to draw up concrete policies relating to the social action programme. Initial consultations between the CEU and the social partners were arranged on the most controversial directive proposals, that is, atypical work contracts, work time, information and hearing, proofs of employment and the securing of national wage and labour condition in connection with cross-national sub-contracting.

Implementing the action programme was brought to a temporary halt at the executive level after a meeting of the labour Ministers Council in November 1990, and a session planned for April 1991 was cancelled. But the first two directives under the Social Charter were adopted on 25 June and both related to health and safety issues. As of 23 December 1993 the Action programme was on track as thirteen out of twenty-five directives had been adopted, nine of which related to health and safety. The remaining four – proof of employment, collective dismissals (changes to directive 75/129/EEC), work time and protection of pregnant women at work – were subsequently approved subject to the procedures stipulated in the Maastricht Treaty. The Pregnancy Directive – which will be subject to detailed inquiry in the following section – was strictly speaking adopted in the framework of 89/391/EEC and as such relates to health and safety. At the same time, however, it is listed in the Charter and social action programme as an equal opportunity initiative.

## 4.2   The Pregnancy Directive

Acting on article 118A of the Single European Act (SEA), directive 90/406/EEC 'concerning the protection at work of pregnant workers or workers who have recently given birth' was adopted by the Social Ministers Council on 19 October 1992. While the directive had originally been proposed under the Social Action Programmes section on 'Equal treatment for men and women', it eventually was passed as the ninth individual directive under the Framework Directive on Health and Safety (89/391/EEC). The directive stipulates minimum rules concerning maternity leave and working conditions of employees who are pregnant or who have recently given birth.

Protecting pregnant women on the job became a CEU ambition in the late seventies. The first Union programme on equal treatment contained provisions to be adopted protecting pregnant women on the job. Although the hazards confronting these women would normally be considered as health and safety related, early deliberations on providing EU regulations protecting pregnant women fell under the auspices of equal treatment whereas none of the early action programmes on health and safety included reference to this issue. However, following the third equality programme with its emphasis on partnership and dialogue, the CEU decided that the directive proposal concerning the protection of pregnant women at work should be related to both the Social Charter – under the heading of equal treatment – and health and safety.[139] This in addition had the advantage of allowing for SEA article 118A to be employed.

Prior to Maastricht most directives proposed under the CEU's Social Action Programme – not defined as health and safety – were subject to unanimous Council voting. This limited the survivability of proposals concerning the social dimension (subject to article 100A as opposed to 118A). In January 1990 the CEU stated that it would attempt to have some of the proposals passed on the basis of article 100 SEA. This article institutes qualified majority voting and was reserved for internal market directives. Differences in labour market conditions should thus be approached as a factor distorting fair competition between member countries. Strong Council objections led the CEU to abandon this strategy and instead redraft whichever proposals possible in a manner placing them under the health and safety heading thus making them subject to article 118A.

Redefining the issue as one relating to health and safety rather than equal treatment caused a recasting of the set as new actors entered the stage. Some organisations refused to accept the new set and left handling of the issue to equal treatment agents which resulted in an asymmetric policy community. The EP thus referred the matter to the hands of the Women's Committee rather than passing it on to the technically and politically far more apt Social Affairs Committee. The CEU's Advisory Committee on equal opportunity was in touch with the process along the way but pursuant to Decision 74/325/EEC, the Advisory Committee on Safety, Hygiene and Health Protection at Work was also consulted and in the corridors of Belaymont it was this Committee which made the strongest impact. This served to some-what alienate the CEU from the EP on the issue.[140] Following the draft stage the CEU, the EP and the Council was to fight a year and a half long fierce political battle over the protection of pregnant women at work.

The CEU first submitted its proposal for a directive to the Council on 18 October 1990. It faced no opposition in the ESC which approved it unanimously on 20 November 1990. A first reading by the EP raised strong criticism of the proposal as the majority of MEPs found the directive much too weak with regard to persons covered, guarantees given and the duration and level of allowances during leave.[141] This caused the CEU to amend its draft and re-submit the proposal to the Council by 3 January 1991. The main changes regarded the inclusion of breastfeeding women.

Disagreement between Council members centred on British and Italian stances representing each extreme. While Italians were discontent with the substance of the directive – it was not considered comprehensive enough in a country traditionally cherishing mother-hood – the British rejected the directive on the grounds of its legal basis. Essentially the UK had a hard time to accept that a directive pertaining to regulate benefits for pregnant women was proposed under an article reserved for health and safety. A full year went before a common position was reached on 19 December 1991. Contrasting Italian and British views were impossible to reconcile and both countries abstained from voting on the common position which was referred to the EP on 14 January 1992. The Italians expected the EP to threaten to turn down the Council position which would grant both the UK and Italy an effective right of veto according to the Cooperation Procedure.

EP deliberations did turn out against the directive which was referred to the Committee on Women's Rights. Two sessions devoted to the common position took place in the EP Committee – on 14 January, the day of receival, and on a double session on 18–19 April 1992. On the recommendation of the Committee, the EP passed a resolution strongly criticising the common position on 17 September 1992. An additional point of criticism was raised concerning the directive's association of pregnancy with sickness. In the following month – just the day before an informal Social Council meeting was scheduled in the UK – a delegation of women met with Belgian Social Minister Mrs Miet Smet in order to exert new pressure on the Council. The above mentioned Council session had been called in order to avoid falling prey to the deadline stipulated in the Cooperation Procedure. The proposal was to expire on 14 October 1992 and the Council was consequently under an immense time pressure.

A compromise was reached in the COREPER shortly after the extension of the deadline. It took two prolonged sessions on 14 and 16 October 1992. As the CEU had abstained from incorporating EP reservations into the directive, it could be adopted using qualified majority. Italy and the UK eventually abstained from voting. The directive was passed on the very day the extended deadline expired.

### 4.3   Equal Opportunity Strategies: From Citizenship to Partnership

Formally, the issues of maternity leave and provisions protecting pregnant women or women who had recently given birth, was brought to the EU agenda amid fear of social dumping. Yet all EU member states maintain national legislation in this field and the EU directive adopted need not have any effect on national legislation. What then was really at stake in relation to the Pregnancy Directive?

In the course of the investigation it was revealed that a new strategy in the field of equal opportunity would be pursued by the CEU relying on partnership and dialogue. The policy process leading up to the Social Charter and the SAP suggests that the CEU considered it useful to advance binding rules as it provides impetus for the social dialogue. Dissent was detected in trade union ranks as national associations seated in the ESC apparently opted for a more minimalist approach than ETUC, which like the CEU had tied up substantial prestige in the dialogue process. As illustrated in the case of the Framework Directive, health and safety issues are increasingly approached in a dialogue manner. The CEU removed the Maternity Directive from the realm of equal opportunity to health and safety. While the Council operates an informal Council on equal opportunity it was at no stage significantly involved in the policy spectacle. Only the EP maintained the issue within the realm of equal opportunity as the Committee on Women Rights stayed firmly in charge of the case during EP deliberations.

By moving the issue from equal opportunity to health and safety the CEU not only enhanced the proposal's survivability enormously as it became subject to qualified majority voting; in addition, it required a much more firm involvement of the social partners who gained access to the policy scene via the upgraded Committee on health, hygiene and safety.

In terms of attempting to improve equal treatment it makes little sense to adopt a directive which only marginally affects existing national legislation. The true impact of the directive has been in involving the social partners in an instance of labour market policy making likely to be concluded with a positive outcome. The whole field of equal opportunity will increasingly rely on cooperation between the social partners. UNICE considers participation feasible if negotiations forbear 'worse' legislation.[142] By linking equal opportunity policy, which owes its solid rooting in the treaties to progressive ECJ rulings, with health and safety subject to qualified majority voting following the ratification of the SEA, employers were put on the defensive.

Besides the impact of French political sponsorship, the EU's legal hierarchy provides a constituency for the state power rationale in relation to equal opportunity. Early colonisation of the EU polity by the state power rationale is reflected in the position of the ECJ and the Union's legal order. Courts are the keepers of individual rights vis-à-vis states and other individuals. The ECJ has practised massive court activism in its progressive interpretation of Treaty provisions mirroring the commitment to individual rights by the Union's juridical sub-system.

Yet with the passing of the Maternity Directive equal opportunity policy has been subjected to a mode of policy making featuring both dialogue and power politics. Basic rights enacted through hierarchical governance structures and founded on basic rights has been replaced by emphasis on: pragmatism (particularly paramount in relation to the legal basis of the directive); institution making (witnessed in relation to the stressing of the dialogue component of the policy field); and 'carrot and stick' tactics as directed against employers forced to lend legitimacy to the dialogue component as outlined above in order to avoid 'unfriendly' legislation in a field powered by a cocktail of court activism and broader institutional spillover mechanisms.

In essence, the state power rationale traditionally underpinning equal opportunity policy has been challenged by contending rationales combining virtues from traditional labour market institutions and money market imperatives such as networking and partnership intrinsic to Catholic social teachings.


## 5   FROM PROTECTION TO PARTICIPATION

Both in the making of European labour market policies and in the execution of policies examined, strong emphasis was placed on establishing frameworks ensuring prolonged and stable patterns of interaction between relevant labour market actors. While the main hurdle facing CEU labour market policy makers remained at times wary of the Council of Ministers, much energy was invested in involving seemingly impotent participants in the process of making and subsequently implementing the policies under consideration. The lack of political powers of the remaining policy actors on the supranational level paired with CEU insistence on their involvement in the process, gives way to the conclusion that the CEU has essentially sought to configure an arena on the supranational level by stimulating direct involvement on the Brussels stage.

By re-configuring national practices via provisions for interaction between labour and management rather than employing participatory baits in the form of substantial regulatory measures, an integrative dynamics has been instituted featuring institutional change strategies going beyond the static political spillover mechanism advanced by neo-functionalists. Systemic transformation is to be achieved by parallel changes at both the domestic and the European level. While the CEU – chiefly represented by the Delors presidency and DGV – has been the architect of the Brussels arena, the French state has provided both political impetus, backing and direct access to Council politicking.

This project signifies a change in the relative penetration of product market and state power rationales vis-à-vis the labour market – and increasingly the money market rationales. Participation and partnership has replaced traditional liberal virtues such as product market transparency and citizenship as chief beacons in the institutional landscape of European labour market integration.

The CEU's prestige and consequent policy impact is subject to alteration as witnessed in relation to the Luxembourg crisis. France hosts a state which displays enormous synchronic coherence – providing it with significant 'real time' political impact – coupled with diachronic incoherence greatly undermining its strategic capacity. Designing and erecting institutions biased towards the desired political-economy design, has consequently been the strategy devised by actors whose current portfolio of preferences are likely to vanish in oblivion as current elites are replaced by successors more strongly influenced by the rationale subject to change. The Social Dimension as an institution-making exercise is reflected even stronger in the attempts of creating European level social dialogue as will be illustrated in the next chapter.

# 4 The Social Dialogue: Creating European Institutions for Labour Market Governance

## 1 INTRODUCTION

Legal provisions regulating labour market affairs, adopted and enacted through formal state agencies, constitute only a part of the total institutional framework of labour markets in European Union member countries.

While labour markets are deeply entrenched in politics, the national agreements reached between employer and employee representatives hovers between a private contractual arrangement and semi-public regulation underpinned by public bodies such as labour courts. National industrial relations systems are thus subject to regimes combining codified legislation, agreements and institutionalised practices regulating both firm level and societal dialogue between the two sides of industry.

Private and public institutions – codified and tacit – combine to create national mixes. These institutional mixes, or macro-level configurations, stipulate the relative position of actors and their organisational division of labour. Macro-level institutional configurations may be dispositioned either towards the realm of the state, contending markets spheres or the genuine labour market rationale as reflected in the neo-corporatist system of intermediation.

In spite of huge diversity in the macro-level configuration of national labour markets, the inter-war period witnessed an increase in the participation of employer and employee organisations in the formal structures of state. In some countries this development was accentuated in the aftermath of the Second World War as social partners were invited to participate in the drawing up of legislation concerning their sphere of interest. State recognition usually followed a period of partial labour market self-regulation. Two or three consecutive conclusions of agreements, without too much public disorder, provided the ticket to state acceptance.[143]

A continuous dialogue between states and social partners thus emerged in political economies identified in the seventies as 'neo-corporatist'. This dialogue has found its most vivid expression in the frameworks for concerted action. Concerted action denotes institutionalised bargaining between social partners and states in which the former moderates its short-term demands in exchange for long-run concessions with regard to future access to, and participation in, general economic policy making.

In concerted action social dialogue transgresses from the sphere of labour market into broader political realms of macroeconomic management. Social dialogue – in the most vivid neo-corporatist formula – is thus an institutionalised mode of societal governance. It stipulates one specific historical form of labour market colonisation, as the ideals held by the associated sphere on the organisation of transaction permeated the spheres of state and markets for money and products.

In this chapter attempts at erecting a system of social dialogue at the European level will be examined. While wage settlements are unlikely to be a topic for European-wide collective bargaining, an extensive system of consultations between the social partners and the CEU has persistently been nurtured. Three distinct historical instances of establishing supranational dialogue institutions are identified, and the political thrust behind their rise and fall are unveiled.

## 2 CREATING COSY TRIANGLES: SOCIAL DIALOGUE AS PLURALIST INTERMEDIATION

Although weak, a social dialogue has existed since the establishment of the Union in 1958. The Treaty of Rome thus contains provisions for the establishment of the Economic and Social Committee (ESC). A forerunner to this body was included in the Treaty of Paris establishing the European Coal and Steel Community.

At the inception of the EU, dominant ideals on both societal governance and integration strategy were incorporated in the design of formal institutions. The fifties decade was the era of behavioural social science reflected in neo-functionalism and its political science stepping stone: pluralist democratic theory.

Pluralist perceptions of political processes attempted to reconcile the normative ideals of classical democratic theory with the disturbing empirical findings of quantitative mass surveys dominant in contemporary American political science. The former thus prescribed a polity resting on an electorate which showed interest in, and was informed about, public affairs. Additionally, high principles and realistic assessments of the 'community interests' – arrived at via discussion and rational reasoning – were propagated as the prevailing traits of the populace. Yet findings on public opinion research indicated that strong sentiments of authoritarianism, prejudice, low levels of tolerance and participation were widespread among the electorate. In addition sociological surveys suggested that voters were anything but the homogenous mass in terms of 'political resources' as assumed by proponents of classical democratic theorists.

Paradoxically, democratic governments continued to nourish, in spite of the above mentioned findings. The low level of participation was increasingly regarded as a proof of the basic soundness of Western political systems. In essence pluralist democratic theory provided ideological legitimacy to political systems characterised by non-coercive elite competition. Elite fragmentation – as reflected in the co-existence of numerous political parties and interest groups – was identified as the defining trait 'polyarchic' systems.

Pluralist democratic theory offered a number of contestable hypotheses regarding the access and participation of certain actor groups.[144] Interest groups are thus supposed to compete for access to policy arenas which in turn are organised as fairly autonomous sectoral triangles bringing together representatives of the former, members of parliament and government bureaucrats. A number of different interest groups may participate at any one time, but as a rule, access is limited and most groups will find themselves out in the cold at one time or another. By picking up the point of early pressure group theories, pluralists contended that neither elected politicians nor pressure groups could alone be regarded as ultimate keepers of power. Hence a complex system of interaction was envisioned which in itself was claimed to hold democratic legitimacy.

As different actors had to interact and bargain before policies could be produced, policy outcome could not simply be reduced to an expression of rationally pursued goals. Incrementalism was the direct result of actor pluralism and the study of decision making became the science of muddling through. Although not one particular actor interest would prevail over the interests of other triangle participants, the nature of pluralist policies was often distributional. As the pluralist definition of politics simply read 'The allocation of goods with value for society', the aim of participants could be reduced to getting their share and preferably a little bit more.

Any policy with a distributional effect would thus attract actors and ensure a cosy triangular pattern of interaction between politicians, bureaucrats and interest groups. These patterns of interaction would have a socialising effect on all three categories of actors which eventually would invest their loyalty in the policy segment rather than anywhere else.

The implications for regional integration strategies seemed straightforward: create a political and administrative framework at the European level, entrust it with some tasks of distributional significance and civil society and markets in the form of organised interests will soon follow suit!

Neo-functionalism thus departed from pluralism. Neo-functionalism in turn became a highly influential body of thinking within corridors of power. While much more pervasive in the Belaymont complex than in the foreign ministries of France and Germany, the general intellectual influence of pluralism and neo-functionalism had the immediate effect of shaping contemporary perceptions of markets and the state – and the interrelation between the two. Catholic thinking, which has left a significant mark on Continental institutional design, was partly discredited by the fact that the losing fascist regimes of Germany – and in particular Italy – had gone some way in associating their ideology with the 'third road' as it was sketchy outlined in various papal documents.[145] Likewise the ramification of the Cold War made the ideological climate hostile for heterodox political economy discourse as this would often share vocabulary with marxism. Hence the parlance of integration in the first years was that of pluralism and its neo-functional offspring. Conceptually this implied a uniform perception of markets, including that for labour. Little attention was directed to its institutional properties. Labour was a production factor which had to submit to mobility alongside goods and capital. Yet in spite of the relative contemporary hegemony of the pure market rationale, the principle of free movement of labour became a stepping stone for a battle-torn institution building process which started immediately after the Rome Treaty came into effect.

## 2.1 The Economic and Social Committee

As discussed in chapter 2, an Economic and Social Committee (ESC) was established in the founding treaties of the European Union. The ESC and its parallel Committee of Representatives in the ECSC, brings together delegates from labour, business, consumers and the professions, in a formal setting which is to act in a consultative capacity vis-à-vis the CEU and the Council.

The inclusion of the ESC in the Treaty of Rome and its predecessor in the Paris Treaty by no means signals that a consensus existed on the nature and future role of this body. While all six founding member states were somewhat familiar with the continental European tradition of Christian Democratic political philosophy with its emphasis on a social market economy, the actual national designs for societal bargaining varied considerably.

Although the EU apparatus inherently stresses formal institutions as preconditions for achieving anything like a socially balanced market economy involving key societal groupings, other factors may precede the erection of European bodies. The Dutch, who in fact operated a comprehensive system of national bargaining based on an institutional set-up bearing close resemblance to the ESC, pointed to the importance of nurturing a political culture prone to consensual politics.[146] The French, by contrast, traditionally emphasise the élan of the national elite's disseminating institutional preferences through the apparatus of state thus forcing remaining societal groupings to fall in line. Also, the German industrial relations system features an 'Economic Council' which provides the setting for intense bargaining in a number of areas. More importantly, however, the country's regionally based wage bargaining system often proves to be the decisive setting for national compromises subsequently implemented by companies which to an exceptional degree involve labour in management.

National experience and aspirations is thus reflected in national positions on institutional design. Besides divergent institutional and strategic preferences, variance could be observed with regard to the overall position of the social partners in the six founding countries. Germany and Benelux thus displayed fairly balanced trade unions and employer associations. France in 'Conseil National du Patronat Français' (CNPF) had a fairly strong employer association while trade unions were weak due to fragmentation.[147] In Italy great regional variations could be observed with the North possessing an industrial relations system similar to that of Germany although ideological cleavages persisted to challenge its stability. As the Rome-based state apparatus repeatedly attempted to link the industrial base of the

North to the less developed South Italian economy, the system was additionally undermined as the forced absorption of the Southern clientalist polity repeatedly introduced profound shocks to the essentially fordist institutional set-up rooted in the economically far more advanced North.[148]

Lacking intergovernmental consensus as to what role the ESC was to perform, was aggravated by dissent between the social partners. Employers thus viewed the EU as primarily a vehicle of mutual market access and tried to reduce questions of social policy to issues relating to geographical mobility of – usually unskilled – workers. The appointment procedures which left it for national governments to choose members did little to persuade national interest groups to commit themselves to Europe. For what it was worth the token of appointment to the ESC was ultimately attributable to national politicking and subsequently the prize could be lost in the national setting as well. This undermined the anticipated transfer of loyalty which in any case rested on the objective foundation that the Union could deliver policies that national governments could not. This was far removed from the realities of early EU social policy which went little beyond the provision of overall guidelines for migrating – usually unskilled – workers.

Having to act in a consultative capacity combined with the presence of the so-called group III (professions and consumers) obviously constrained the ESC's ability to offer a setting for social dialogue. In addition ESC seats are allotted by member states leaving little room for employees and business to assemble coherent delegations.

As a setting for social dialogue the ESC failed partly because it did not provide a suitable framework – size and composition, reflecting divergent national preferences with regard to the role of the body saw to that – and partly because the right actors were not in place – trade unions still had some way to go before anything pertaining to be a European platform was in operation and UNICE did everything to avoid having to face social issues at the EU level – and finally there really was not much to conduct a dialogue on as the EU had no thorough competencies in the field and national labour market systems in some member states were still in the making.

## 2.2 Sectoral Social Dialogue: The Joint Committees

As the apparent shortcomings of the ESC reduced it to merely a consultative body, proponents of stronger EU social policy involvement resorted to the so-called joint committees – an organisational newcomer invented for the occasion.

'Committeeology' is the term coined by the CEU to ridicule the Council's practice of establishing committees entrusted with the task of monitoring the activities of the CEU. The CEU has, however, established its own extensive network of committees which are to advise the Commission on given subjects. Besides the ESC, COREPER and the vast amount of sub-committees serving these two bodies, essentially four categories of EU-level committees can be identified. In many respects, the most powerful of these are the so-called 'management committees' which overlook the CEU's implementation of EU policies. They mainly operate in fields where the Union hands out grants or quotas as in the case of agriculture, R&D and fisheries policies. The terms 'consultative' and 'advisory' committees are often used interchangeably. Functionally they are identical but committees carrying the label 'consultative' are often appointed by the Council whereas advisory committees are commissioned by the CEU. Their role is to offer sectoral expert advice to mainly CEU on given issues.[149] 'Joint committees' constitute the third category which besides offering advice in principle are expected to conclude agreements constituting a regulatory component in a given field. 'Informal committees' is the final category. They resemble joint committees with respect to composition and purpose and, while in no official way affiliated to the formal EU bodies, they receive roughly the same practical and economic assistance as formal joint committees.

A number of consultative committees serve as forums of social dialogue. As opposed to joint and informal committees consultative committees are established by the Council and comprise national representatives of trade unions, employer associations and civil servants usually appointed on the basis of expert status.[150]

Advisory committees established by the CEU are occasionally set up in response to requests from European associations; this is particularly the case at the intermediary level. When the CEU is responsible for appointing members to an advisory committee, members are usually drawn from European associations. In bodies where the Council appoint members, representatives of various national organisations are generally occupying the bulk of seats.[151]

The Council has appointed thirteen committees including the ESC, the advisory committee on transport, the ECSC advisory committee and the Tripartite Conference discussed later. The CEU in turn has created eight joint committees and seven advisory committees.[152] As of today no complete directory or similar source accessible to the general public regarding consultative committees exist. [153]

The joint committees essentially bring together the two sides of industry in a given sector on a parity basis. It was the CEU which took the initiative of establishing these committees and in addition sponsor much of their activity. Formal joint committees have been set up in agriculture (1963), road transport (1965), inland waterway transport (1967), sea fishing (1968) and rail transport (1971).

As dialogue progress came to a standstill in the course of the seventies, the CEU started to nurture the creation of committees outside the formal auspices of the Union. These committees – also composed of representatives from intermediary European associations – operate with a less ambitious set of objectives. Rather than being pressured by the official expectation of constituting a negotiation setting, members meet regularly – not necessarily on parity bases – to exchange views on important problems within their sector.[154]

Joint committee delegates are drawn from intermediary European associations. These European level interest groups are usually smaller than the more comprehensive European confederations. Often understaffed and underfunded they have been living in the shadow of UNICE, ETUC and predecessors of the latter. Their affiliation with European confederations vary from no formal attachment on the side of employers to integrated hierarchical structures on the side of trade unions. Organisational structures may, however, become more uniform as UNICE is attempting to establish a joint employer platform. Joint committees contain between 38 and 50 members and the chair rotates every second year. Generous assistance is offered by the CEU with respect to planning meetings and providing locations, interpretation and general secretarial aid.

While the intended role of joint committees was ambitious the bulk of their work has been to conduct studies and provide expert input on health and safety regulation. Something on the nature of a collective agreement has been reached within the auspices of joint committees as employers and employees of the agricultural sector in 1978 and 1980 concluded a formal deal on working hours within crop farming and horticulture.

As most domestic interest groups on both sides of industry usually left it up to national confederations to handle EU affairs, only limited resources were devoted by constituent associations in the European joint committees. In particular employers were very reluctant to commit themselves too strongly to European-wide solutions. In some important sectors such as shipbuilding, the motor industry, construction, textiles and the chemical industries no joint committees have been established due to strong reservations from the employers.[155]

Informal joint committees have been set up in banking, construction, retail, hotel/catering, machine tools, shipbuilding, insurance and telecommunication. Banking and construction have been close to actually concluding agreements within the introduction of new technologies (banking) and vocational training (construction).[156]

It is striking that the two most mature sectoral dialogues – agriculture and banking – takes place within sectors which have benefited most directly from the European Union. The fate of most European agricultural producers is inevitably tied to the Common Agricultural Policy (CAP); without external tariffs and high levels of subsidies North American producers would dominate the market. Banking has traditionally been constrained by tight national regulation. The sector was the first area were the benefits of the internal market scheme was reaped which is the key in understanding the credit based economic boom of the latter part of the eighties.[157]

## 2.4    The First Phase of Social Dialogue: Societal Governance through State Intervention

As the majority of the Union's 'founding fathers', pointing to the 1954 ILO report, were largely dismissive of conducting European level labour market policies, proponents of such a venture would have to rely on other mechanisms than the painstaking process of institution building via intergovernmental negotiations. Hence allowing room for the political involvement of interest groups in the EU policy making process, may be regarded as the concession given to 'maximalists' in return for highly deluded treaty provisions on labour market policy.

High hopes were consequently placed on emerging neo-functional theories pertaining to explain integrative dynamics. As already pointed out emphasis on this influential body of thinking was on elite socialisation. By constructing a setting bringing together representatives of European labour and business it was assumed that European solutions to labour market problems would eventually be devised.

The neo-functional logic of technical (economic) spillover transgressing into political spillover assumed a pluralist polity to be in operation featuring collective organised economic interests geared at influencing the political system. This image of a political 'superstructure' dictated by an economic 'base' had special appeal to analysts of labour markets. Hence as the common market included labour and capital there were good reasons to expect political pressure from labour to standardise labour market regulation.

In creating the ESC, mounting societal pressure was apparently anticipated. Accordingly the creation of the ESC was part of a constitutional struggle in which dominant actors incorporated societal groupings not directly participating in the initial design process. Advocates of comprehensive European integration could, backed by neo-functionalists, claim a victory as the making of the ESC opened the 'lid' for organised interests and hence an automatic expansion of scope fuelled by spillover mechanisms.

Yet adherents to a more restricted and marked oriented approach to European integration could equally claim success as the free flow of goods and capital, according to conventional economic theory constitutes a substitute to international labour migration.[158] As labour mobility in addition is constrained by cultural and lingual barriers, the Union at an early stage apparently opted for relying on economic transfers to disadvantaged regions by means of the regional-structural funds, rather than leaving it to the market to re-allocate labour from regions backsliding in response to free trade to regions prospering in the face of enhanced market opportunities.

In hindsight, essentially three different roles could be performed by the ESC. First, it could serve as an arena of direct negotiations between key societal groupings subject to monitoring or supervision by the executive. As such the body would adhere to what has been labelled state-sponsored corporatism. Secondly, it could serve as a venue point for key societal groupings and the executive. Deals concluded elsewhere could formally be brought forward to the executive for either acceptance or amendment. Such an arrangement would conform to the con-societal form of corporatism. Thirdly, a mode of operation could be envisioned which allotted to the ESC the task of serving the executive bodies of the Union in a 'societal advisory capacity'. As such the set-up would correspond to the weak forms of 'tri-partism' practised in the seventies by, for example, the UK. As EU labour market policy objectives were vague and disputed at the time of the ESC's creation, the main function of the body was to add legitimacy to the newly formed supranational system.

Theoretically the legacy of neo-functionalism with its implicit application of pluralist democratic theory is evident. Although access to a number of settings was granted by the Council and the CEU, a basic belief in competition is reflected in the heterogeneity of actors admitted to the ESC. The sectoral dialogues appear somewhat more neo-corporatist at first glance. However, the initiation of sectoral arenas with no co-ordinating superstructure bears evidence of a prevailing theoretical outlook featuring classic pluralist segmentation.

Political science and political economy of this first phase of European social dialogue was based on common intellectual ground reflected in the perception of the state and the market. Pluralists regarded the state as central to all political calculation while political economists portrayed the state as the central institution of market economies. Hence pluralist theories of policy making featuring an image of the distributional (weak) or programmatic (strong) state subject to external pressure from interest groups, could easily be accommodated to the findings of political economy.

Traces of both the pure market and the state power rationales can be detected during this first phase of European social dialogue. The pluralist element points partly to pure market thinking as it generally emphasises competition in politics and hence aligns neatly with the economic practice as prescribed by this rationale. Pluralism, however, also bases itself on the assumption that markets can be governed, centrally, by political means. Policies of redistribution are the hallmarks of pluralist polities. Wealth is redistributed to maintain societal equilibrium and maximise welfare. Pluralism essentially claims that politics *can* allocate wealth in society. This presupposes a positive belief in the societal prerogatives of states – while likely to be deemed naive by current observers – well attuned to the creeds of the state power rationale. The spillover concept is less ambiguous in its predisposition vis-à-vis the identified rationales. Spillover implies a state market dichotomy elevating the latter to the prime source of societal dynamics.

Two components constitute the dialogue efforts of the first phase. The ESC was established in a constitutional game involving heads of states and governments, foreign secretaries and their respective civil services. From its inception the ESC was equipped with an ambiguous set of tasks. Some of the founding member states held the expectations that the body was to serve as subordinate to the Council in a governance system rooted in the state power rationale. At the time of the Union's creation only the central actors of states were involved in the negotiation and hence the institutional design process. Accordingly settings were constructed with a state power bias regardless of the overall balance of contending rationales in

member countries. In subsequent attempts to fill out the organisational framework left by the first Inter-Governmental Conference,
neither the social partners nor the remaining organisations, formal or
informal, managed to infuse autonomous societal thrust into the
body – the ESC was too entrenched in the state power rationale to
resurrect as a genuine venue of social dialogue.

The sectoral dialogues were initiated and sponsored by the CEU.
They were designed in accordance with pluralist doctrines. No states
were actively involved at this venture, and the implied mixed state
power and pure market rationales reflected the strong grip neo-functionalist ideology had on the CEU.[159]

As evident, pluralist strategies for developing the social dialogue
proved unsuccessful. Labour markets and the accompanying political
superstructure did not conform to pluralist interest group ideals and
polyarchic patterns of interaction. Neo-corporatist literature
captured contemporary elite ideals on the role of labour markets in
overall societal governance. As neo-corporatist thinking challenged
pluralism in university corridors, policy practicians, engaged in the
design of Europe's political economy, employed the new paradigm in
the set up of arenas and institutions replacing the 'triangular' and
fragmented venues stemming from the original neo-functional
construct.

## 3 CREATING CORPORATISM – THE DISHARMONIES OF EUROPEAN CONCERT

With the 'relaunch' of the Union, following the show-down between
Walther Hallstein and Charles de Gaulle, initial moves were made to
upgrade social aspects of integration. Meeting under the auspices of
the then informal European Council, the French head of state and the
five heads of government managed to set the direction for the future
development of the rapidly faltering integration process. At the 1969
Hague summit the Union was facing widespread social unrest and a
new French presidency which with unease observed an international
re-orientation of an equally new German administration. New issues
were badly needed as most of the original aims had already been
achieved. The new project was to be Economic and Monetary Union
(EMU) preferably in combination with closer foreign policy cooperation.[160]

With EMU vital domestic policy instruments were to be transferred to the European level. This transfer was to take place in a time where trade unions, together with employer associations, had been successful in gaining privileged access to economic policy making. From the perspectives of states, moving power centres of national economic management from domestic arenas, in which key societal groupings had access, to supranational arenas were the very same groupings had hardly organised, could inflict a loss of political legitimacy far greater than that experienced during the May 1968 riots. It was, in addition, likely to produce a change of discursive equilibrium in national political economies practising neo-corporatism in one form or another. Arrangements of concerted action consequently implied a colonisation of the money market sphere by the labour market rationale. If markets for money were to be re-constituted at the European level, where labour had virtually no institutional footing, national re-configuration seemed inevitable unless national labour market spheres joined and elevated their constituencies.

In the early seventies pluralism was increasingly blamed for portraying inadequately the roles of interest groups and states in the policy process. This critique was ultimately aimed towards pluralist assumptions about the distribution of power in western societies. Neo-corporatism was originally suggested as a contesting view on the role of interest groups in mainly West European polities.[161] It pointed to a unified mode of policy making as all major domestic decisions in society were linked together in grand bargains at the top level.[162]

Neo-corporatist critics of pluralism rejected the view of interest groups competing for access at the input level of the political system. Rather a 'continuous, structured participation of interest organisations in the policy making (and sometimes policy implementation) process'[163] was envisaged. It followed that interest organisations were not merely performing functions of interest aggregation. The traditional image of group member interests being aggregated and eventually communicated to relevant agencies by agents at the top level, was replaced with the notion of a two-dimensional demand flow with one being the traditional member/top flow and another going from agents to members. The member socialisation assumption reflects the contractual nature of corporatism.[164] Radical proponents of corporatism envisioned a state-societal interest dichotomy with states dominating societal interests. This domination did not have the blunt appearance found in authoritarian regimes, rather it was a subtle manipulative strategy based on the co-optation of organised interests, that is, making interest organisations co-responsible for

state policies. In return for continuous and structured policy participation, interest organisations had to deliver member support for
policy outputs – or at least suppress member resistance.[165]

The purpose of domination was to ensure the long-term interests
of the state. Incidentally, the second major point of criticism was
directed towards pluralist perceptions of the state. Early pluralists
concept of polyarchy contended that political decisions were made by
a range of competitive elites fragmented across issue areas.
Government decisions were indirectly constrained significantly by the
majority through electoral competition. Although civil servants
participated in the decision making process, they did not define
themselves as belonging to a group with common interests pursuing
the interests of the state or the civil service at large. Their interests
were directed towards issue areas and constituted a segment of a
fragmented elite. Thus pluralism was a stateless theory. Adherents to
continental European polity traditions strongly opposed this *laissez-
faire* perception of policy making. Scholars of especially Marxist
observance resorted to the rapidly expanding body of state theory
sparked off by, in particular, French and German political philoso-
phers like Althusser, Poulantzas and Hirch. They perceived the
bourgeois state as the institutional reflection of the capitalist mode
of production. A central theme of dispute was the degree of autonomy endured upon the apparatus of state from the capitalist class.
Theoretical convergence, however, prevailed on the view that states
long-term interests coincided with the interests of the capitalist class.
This conveying of an ultimate purpose on the state as distinct from
government had drastic theoretical consequences. For once the
incremental nature of decision making put forward by pluralists had
to be severely qualified, since incrementalism could hardly be
expected to fulfil a long-term pre-defined purpose. Secondly, the
notion of a fragmented and departmentalised state presumably falls
short of meeting the coordination requirements for achieving state-
wide collective end-goals.

Neo-corporatism challenged the assumption about who governed
and the nature of policy outcomes. In terms of actors the state, as an
entity encompassing the central bureaucracy and the executive, rose
to prominence together with what was considered leading economic
interest groups in capitalist society: labour and industry. Neo-corporatism was observed as a simultaneous historical and contemporary
phenomenon by Schmitter in his 1974 article. In later works he and
Wolfgang Streeck viewed neo-corporatism more as a strategy pursued

by certain West European governments in the wake of the 1970s world recessions.[166] Neo-corporatism can historically be considered an ideological companion to the labour market rationale. Social force mobilised by antagonist societal groupings determines political struggles on growth and distribution policies.

Hence at the peak of neo-corporatism in key member states unprecedented attention was paid to labour issues. As the Customs Union – and free movement of labour – took legal effect in 1968, social issues gradually reappeared on the EU agenda.[167] This ramified into European politics reflected in discussions on employment services, vocational guidance and occupational training at the first informal Council of Europe which eventually agreed to convene a Tripartite Conference.

### 3.1    The Tripartite Conferences

Dissatisfaction with the ESC prompted the social partners to request the Council to establish a tripartite setting where employment issues could be discussed. This joint initiative reflected distrust with CEU conduct of emergent EU labour policy rather than consensus on what type of labour market issues were to be addressed at the Union level.

A joint letter was forwarded to the President of the Council on 9 May 1968 followed by a letter from the two main European trade unions on 18 October 1968. Little has been reported on the reply of the Council. As the Council can do very little between sessions it is of no surprise that it was the CEU which stepped in and persuaded the social partners to elaborate on their request, at a meeting taking place in Luxembourg in November 1969.

Dissatisfaction was caused by the disappointing performance of the ESC which had deteriorated to an extent where not even the CEU bothered to use the body for anything but compulsory consultation. As the CEU in addition had invested substantial political prestige on sectoral dialogues, peak organisations were anxious to get hold of the Union's handling of labour market affairs which was widely expected to be boosted by the completion of the Customs Union. Though a genuine and widespread desire existed among the social partners to establish some form of dialogue, they were incapable of embarking on a path of negotiations without CEU tutelage. This prompted the latter to convene a conference on social dialogue.

The conferences were tri-partied only in the terminology of the EU. Besides the social partners and the CEU, the Labour Affair

Ministers – and eventually Ministers of Finance – of each of the member states were present. Convening for the first time in 1970, these conferences where repeated until 1978 when ETUC, claiming they had lost patience with the slow progress of the negotiations, abandoned the talks.

Meeting in Luxembourg in 1970, the main outcome of the first Tripartite Conference was the setting up of a Standing Committee on Employment (SCE). Calls for the creation of such a committee were made in 1967 by Christian trade unions, and received backing from the UNICE. The committee still exists and still encompasses representatives from member states, the social partners and the CEU.

Only after express support was given to the Tripartite Conferences following the 1974 summit did the dialogue gain momentum. Following the second meeting on 16 December 1974 substantial issues were placed on the agenda including the impact of the economic recession on the quantity and quality of employment and equal treatment. The third conference – convened on 18 November 1975 – was devoted to finding European solutions to rising levels of unemployment. A fourth conference was held 24 June 1976 and successfully concluded with a joint statement expressing the intention of participants to strive for gradual reduction of inflation rates to 4–5 per cent and boost annual GDP growth levels to 5 per cent! The fifth conference held 17 June 1977 under the banner 'growth, stability and employment' presented participants with the fact that economic development had paid little attention to their delicately crafted conclusion at the previous meeting. The sixth meeting which commenced on 9 November 1978 concentrated on the question of redistributing available employment. No conclusion, let alone decisions, were achieved and the social partners, via the ESC, declared that future participation would depend upon concrete proposals being submitted and adopted. In addition, ETUC bluntly stated that they had no intention of participating in future Conferences if they were to be conducted in a similar manner.

Facing these threats the CEU submitted a series of proposals to the social partners and the Council. As frustration was mainly present on the side of employees, no consensus on the CEU's initiative was achieved between the social partners. In addition member states – represented by the Council – were wary of transferring competence in overall macroeconomic management to the tripartite conferences which in any case were hampered by excessive usage of empty rhetoric, antagonist attitudes and lacking cohesion among, in particular, labour and state participants. The Council eventually responded in 1980 by advancing a timid set of guidelines regarding the conduct and goals of the conferences which in combination with the complete lack of consensus produced the final breakdown of the dialogue. The Tripartite Conference has thus not been convened since the 1978 session.

Alongside negotiations held at the Tripartite Conferences a more low salient dialogue was conducted in the SCE. It involved the national Minister of Labour from the country holding the Council presidency, the CEU and the social partners. In a sense this setting can be compared to the joint committees although it brings together peak organisations rather than representatives of intermediary associations. While the inclusion of the CEU and the Social Policy (Labour Minister) Council made the SCE appear potent, confusion has persisted as to its goals and instruments. Formally the objective of the SCE is:

> to ensure close contact at the Community level between the Social Partners, so as to facilitate the coordination of the employment policies of the member states by harmonising them with Community objectives.

The operations of the SCE gave impetus to a number of dramatic conflicts between trade unions and employers and, more importantly, in the trade unions' own ranks. As the SCE was a direct product of the Tripartite Conferences it made little sense to try to track down the dynamics of its creation. Interestingly, however, the rows stemming from the constitution of the committee can serve to puncture the image of a European social dialogue being established as a result of strong pressures from key societal groupings acting on the basis of predetermined historical trajectories. The trade union side – supposedly pushing for social progress at the EU level – was in no way ready to face the challenge of acting cohesively. Dominant national trade union centres, bound by their different domestic experiences, were unable to provide the leadership necessary to utilise the access granted to the EU social policy community. As no supranational leadership at the time could be identified on the side of trade unions, open conflict broke out between national and competing supranational labour delegates.

The amalgamation of the socialist 'European Confederation of Free Trade Unions' (EUFTU) and the Christian 'European

Organisation of the World Confederation of Labour' (EO-WCL) in 1973 only marked the beginning of a long process which was needed to reconcile divergent philosophies of European trade unionism. While European trade unions have often been pointed to as a central force pushing for social dialogue at the EU level, they did not constitute an actor performing a meaningful role in a dialogue setting created by the CEU.

It is plausible that the European trade union movement was unaware of their institutional shortcomings or, alternatively, hoped external pressure could help them overcome it. The latter presumes that some consensus existed between the two European level peak organisations, and that this consensus, however tacit, could be combined in some joint strategic exercise. This seems highly unlikely given the row that broke in the aftermath of the creation of the SCE. The former option, that unions were ignorant of the organisational strains and challenges posed when entering social dialogue, seems equally unlikely given the experiences of constituent national organisations. Either pressure has to be found outside trade unions or labour bearers of dialogue constitute a sub-group of actors within the ranks of organised workers – for example, Brussels based labour movement professionals.

### 3.2 The Second Phase of Social Dialogue: Societal Governance through Co-option of Organised Markets

Given the role played by the CEU in setting up in particular sectoral dialogues and the Tripartite Conferences – in addition to the set of interests held by other actors – it must be concluded that the initiation of dialogue has primarily been sponsored by the CEU which managed to gain support from the European level social partners. National constituent organisations remained more cautious in their enthusiasm.

The CEU managed to obtain express support from member states unable to pursue a policy of dialogue in their domestic setting due to severe shortcomings in their institutional configurations. In sum, the efforts of the second phase are best understood as an attempt at extending the neo-corporatist practice of certain member states to the supranational level. The agenda, aim and design of the setting clearly reflects neo-corporatist aspirations.

As the CEU could not endogenously generate a momentum in the making of labour market policy legislation sufficiently vivid to attract key societal groupings at the Brussels arena, it reversed the neo-functional logic of integration and created a setting for the social partners – hoping some policies would be produced requiring minimal codification. Rather than relying on bottom-up mechanisms implied in pluralist democratic theory, the CEU resorted to the 'statist' remedies of classical state-sponsored corporatism by devising centrally constructed settings inhabited with largely centrally constructed actors.

Diminishing dependence on formal EU policy making was attractive since labour issues hitherto had fallen outside the scope of the Union's legal basis. Had this strategy been pursued with Council consent it would been likely to involve an expansion of the legal competence of the Union so as to include labour market policy thus ensuring participation of the social partners at the European level. This has to some extent happened with the coming into effect of the Maastricht treaty. This growing salience of EU labour market policy has, however, been achieved by pointing to an 'artificial' societal pressure sponsored by the CEU, and substantial advances in the field still depends on the active support from the Council.

Labour market policy issues are raised to prominence on the agenda following a cyclical pattern. Whenever major initiatives enjoying high priority among member states are launched, the CEU manages to squeeze in labour market policy. The Council, eager to demonstrate unity around high profile endeavours, let this pass because an inter-organisational conflict could harm its own agenda. The CEU usually attempts to pair labour market policy initiatives with the establishment of social dialogue in anticipation of Council resistance whenever ambitious labour market policy statements are to be transformed into legislation. Limited legal competencies in the field of labour market policy thus in itself provides stimulus to CEU attempts of creating a European level social dialogue.

Proponents of social dialogue in the seventies included actors naturally biased for solutions on the Union level and groups denied access in their domestic settings. Yet a number of member states had only started to erect neo-corporatist structures at the national level. These attempts posed severe challenges to states as well as national social partners. While a rationale could undoubtedly be identified for transgressing these arrangements to the supranational level – for example, globalisation of the economy, money market prominence – only few states possessed the required institutional capacity at the domestic level thus rendering prospects of successfully pursuing similar strategies on a European level hopeless. Member states had in addition already demonstrated their reluctance to transfer too many competencies to the supranational level.

Hence states had few incentives to accept a transfer of core competencies, concerning macroeconomic management, to institutionally poorly equipped European peak organisations. A similar logic applies to the social partners. Organisations successful in achieving access to governments in their domestic base had little reason to go to Brussels as the Council held the upper hand in EU policy making – especially in broad issues areas such as economic policy.

Intensified political integration is frequently justified by economic necessity. While such reasoning had some credence, national policy – ultimately resting on states' domestic capacity – decisively affected the economic fortune of individual countries during the oil crises and the accompanying recessions. While differences in economic structure and factor endowments vis-à-vis new market demands offered both constraints and opportunities for economic strategies, states exercised considerable measurements of control on national economic development. This capacity varied with the institutional set-up and political culture of individual states. Some countries thus navigated more successfully through the crises than others. In the EU, Germany, Holland and France managed to fend off the repercussion of recession better then the United Kingdom, Italy and Belgium even though no clear pattern of differences in economic structures can be identified between the two groups of countries. Variations in terms of basic institutional features reflects more accurately differences between countries coping either tolerably or disastrously with crises. In general, the better performing countries achieved more consistent and balanced participation of national social partners in economic policy making or – as in the case of France – managed to exploit fading state prerogatives to the limit.

Divisions in state interests could plausibly materialise as institutionally weaker countries might opt for a strategy of re-configuration. Essentially these states could choose to devise a European approach enforcing institutional harmonisation, hence ensuring the 'cruder' political economies societal properties matching those of the more successful member countries.

Countries featuring successful neo-corporatist structures by contrast stood to lose their advantages as a pooling of sovereignty at both the level of state and at the level of the social partners would inevitably produce asymmetry with regards to the size of the stakes.

Successful neo-corporatist political economies thus faced the risk of losing national managerial prerogatives in exchange for a share in a supranational governance system characterised by great uncertainty.

Logically this should place France, Italy and the United Kingdom in the category of member states favouring dialogue. Ideological cleavages have, however, blurred the coalition pattern of states promoting or resisting European dialogue. In any case states possessing weakly founded institutional configurations were in a very bad position to initiate or sponsor a European social dialogue, as they had no access to strong national trade union centres or national employer federations prone to dialogue.

One keen proponent of European social dialogue – the CEU – did enjoy privileged access to trade union and employer association representatives somewhat prone to European dialogue. This privileged access rested on the fact that the European trade union organisation(s) were largely sponsored by the CEU while the relative positive attitude of European level employer representatives were prompted by the implicit bargain proposed – an even more liberal European market place in return for a social dimension. Yet supranational leadership was weak at the time and trade unions especially had insisted on attendance of Economic and Finance Ministers at the Tripartite Conferences as well as at the SCE. This stemmed from recognition of the fact that at the EU level, social partners could achieve little on their own and that the CEU had lost authority and political prestige since the convening of the first summits.

The Tripartite Conferences were thus half-hearted in any sense of the word. It was brought forward by a CEU paralysed by the ramifications of Luxembourg and stalemated by internal Council grievances following enlargement. It received modest support from European social partners at an embryonic stage of development. Labour and industrial relations branches of business associations were thus only beginning to discover the EU arena as a potentially potent labour market policy setting.

The truly puzzling aspect of the second stage of the European social dialogue is consequently not why it failed but rather how it managed to materialise at all. Rather than being promoted by strong, committed actors following a coherent strategy the relative durability of social dialogue in the second phase was a result of contemporary dominant discourses on governance firmly rooted in certain member states and on the advance in remaining EU countries. In the seventies the labour market rationale thus had a good grip of the political economies of Germany, Italy, the Low Countries and Denmark. It in addition challenged dominant rationales in France and Britain. While the dialogue strategy was carried forth by no substantial political forces other than what could be mustered by a generally disillusioned CEU, it was not met with consistent resistance either. It was in accordance with national developments and hence not subject to ideological challenges. It was, however, largely incompatible with national developments as the implied concerted action strategies of neo-corporatism are inherently chauvinist.[168]

The second phase demonstrates the autonomy of EU organisations such as the CEU which can act with considerable discretion when in tune with dominant discourse. It also amply illustrates that the EU is far from being a genuine super-state. While the CEU and similar organisations possess substantial autonomy in the policy process, member states remain key actors in casting the European polity.


4  A NEGOTIATED GROWTH STRATEGY: FROM VAL DUCHESSE TO EGMONT PALACE

In 1985 the social dialogue was revived with the convening of a series of meetings at the Val Duchesse Castle outside Brussels. As opposed to the Tripartite Conferences these meetings were not attended by Ministers from member states.

Up through the eighties, following the increasingly ideologically charged – and futile – debate between pluralists and neo-corporatists, the negotiated approach to national economic management was rediscovered by academics moving the locus of inquiry away from the apparatus of state towards socio-institutional features.[169] The school in particular took off in Norway and Denmark.[170] It departed from the state-centred approach of early neo-corporatism and stressed the important role of relatively autonomous societal actors like trade unions and business associations in forming the national economic discourse. In line with Kenneth Dyson, who had stressed the notion of an industrial culture associated with society at large rather than merely the state bureaucracy, the understanding of societal governance advocated by proponents of the negotiated economy approach was broadened to include negotiated settlements by peak societal organisations involving a wide range of bearers of public authority.

The negotiated approach constituted a departure from the pre-occupation with formal institutions. Various segments of public bodies and venues were thus grouped under functional headings according to their role in the discourse formation process.

Emphasis is on the making of a common understanding of key societal issues and a jointly identified plethora of solutions informed by the collective diagnosis. This is achieved via direct interaction between key actors as well as through the media. By focusing on the old Gramscian notion of discourse formation, proponents of the negotiated approach, shifted attention from the closing of specific corporatist bargains to the formation of overall 'regimes' within which deals are to be struck. As the 'regime' or overall intellectual climate more or less determines the character of these deals, it is argued that the most crucial choices are made in the preceding discourse formation process rather than at the neo-corporatist negotiating tables.

Corresponding to the changing emphasis of political economy, the literature on interest intermediation has shifted its locus of inquiry from fairly transparent organisational structures, featuring peak interest groups, towards more flexible structures on the meso-level. A common denominator between contemporary political economy and political science thus seems to be the concepts and terminology of the policy network approach.

In a major theoretical contribution Patrick Kenis and Volker Schneider[171] contend that with the advent of the policy network terminology the focus of societal governance has moved from hierarchical control systems to horizontal co-ordination. It is the character of the actors, and the nature of their mutual interaction, that constitute the defining traits of policy networks. And the functioning and composition of policy networks in turn constitute an important institutional property of political economies. The impact on societal governance strategies is monumental as the token of bargaining no longer is the passive consent of vast numbers of rank and file, but active support and promotion of policy discourses by key opinion makers with access to rank and file. Governance strategies stressing network creation and discourse formation thus replace mass mobilisation power. Hence the ability to monopolise and display 'valid' knowledge, and the overall information dissemination capacity of actors, becomes vital power prerogatives.[172]

The direct high level dialogue of the Val Duchesse setting is aimed at producing agreements between trade unions and employer associations with the CEU serving as inspiration and mediator. The latter has consequently managed to bypass governmental reservations for common European labour market rules expressed by certain members of the Council.

The March 1987 meeting at Val Duchesse produced one of the first tangible results as participants agreed on a joint statement on vocational training in connection with the implementation of new technologies and procedures concerning employee information and consultation rights.[173] Another breakthrough took place in September 1990 when the first collective agreement was reached at the European level between ETUC and the European Centre of Public Enterprises (CEEP).[174] The dialogue first peaked, however, when on 3 October 1991 the social partners agreed on an accord defining their future role in the making of EU labour market policy. This agreement was accordingly incorporated into the Maastricht Treaty by the intergovernmental conference on the European Union and today assumes the status of EU constitutional law!

Three types of agreements – or joint opinions – have thus far been reached. One set of joint opinions concerns concrete problems such as guidelines on the hearing and consultation of workers in connection with the implementation of new technologies. This category of agreements bears resemblance to national negotiated labour law as typically found in the Scandinavian countries. A second group of agreements encompass rather more broad statements of macroeconomic goal setting at the Union level. This clearly gives association to the neo-corporatist set-ups dominating in particular Germany in the seventies. Finally, a third type of agreement has been produced which aims at defining the scope for joint action by the social partners in the Union framework. The joint opinion adopted at Egmont Palace on 3 October 1991 is the only instance of such an agreement but it is at the same time by far the most significant deal reached between the two sides of industry at the European level.

### 4.1 Towards a European Industrial Relations System?

Observers stressing continuity in the evolution of European social dialogue date the origins of the Val Duchesse talks to the joint meeting between Ministers of Financial Affairs and Ministers for Employment and Social Affairs on 16 November 1982. Noting that the set of rules drawn up at the 1980 Social Council session relating to the Tripartite Conferences had not been sufficient to rejuvenate the setting, the need for close and sustained cooperation between the two sides of industry was stressed.[175] The meeting was the second of the so-called 'jumbo meetings' convened at the request of especially the ETUC.[176] Appeals for arriving at social consensus through dialogue at the Union level were repeated at most subsequent Social Council meetings.[177] Particularly explicit at the Social Council meeting of 22 June 1984, where a second medium term social action programme was adopted containing provisions which left it up to the CEU to revive the social dialogue.

Pressure leading to this decision had apparently been brought to bear by the ETUC which had taken the lead as it convened a conference on employment on 5 April 1984 in Strasbourg, inviting among others the President of the Council, French Première Pierre Mauroy, several other heads of government and the President and Vice-President of the CEU.[178] The outcome of the conference was a series of appeals for increased dialogue from trade union, Council and CEU representatives. Similar calls for intensified dialogue were made by the UNICE which in the same month submitted a leaflet to candidates running for the upcoming EP elections stressing the need for dialogue between workers and employers 'to bring job supply and demand more into line.'[179]

Joint pressure from the social partners and the Council demanding moves be made to intensify the dialogue process can thus be observed. The signals were readily received by the CEU which produced an article in its official conveyor on EU labour market policy news 'Social Europe' which summarised the situation as above.[180]

Soon after taking office as CEU's new President in January 1985 Jacques Delors informally approached the social partners at a joint session at the Val Duchesse Castle outside Brussels. These contacts resulted in the first formal Val Duchesse meeting on 12 November 1985. The meeting brought together Mr Delors, Mr Pfeiffer and Mr Sutherland of the CEU and all Chairmen and General Secretaries of organisations affiliated to the UNICE, CEEP and ETUC.[181]

At the first formal meeting the partners had already been reconciled to an extent enabling them to adopt the first joint opinion on the broad lines for a cooperative growth strategy. Following this statement, a working party comprised of representatives of the social partners and the CEU was set up to monitor the economic and employment situation with a view to a more in-depth discussion of the CEU's Annual Economic Report. In addition to the joint statement on the cooperative growth strategy, a joint declaration of intent was adopted expressing the willingness of the partners to work towards producing a joint opinion on the introduction of new technologies. To this end a restricted working party was established.[182]

Two joint opinions were adopted by the macroeconomic working party and one by the working party on new technology prior to the review meeting at Egmont Palace on 7 May 1987. All parties confirmed their commitment to the dialogue and for the first time the meeting was attended by the Council Presidency – represented by Mr Wilfried Martens of Belgium – who pledged that the joint opinions already adopted would be put before the European Council at the June 1987 summit. This was followed up by a joint telegram submitted by ETUC, UNICE and CEEP to the Copenhagen summit in December 1987. The telegram concerned the budget crisis and related the issue with the cooperative growth strategy outlined in the joint opinions of the macroeconomic working party. The telegram was signed by the General Secretaries of the European secretariats of the three associations.[183]

At this stage the social partners had been represented only by domestic executives – one from each EU member state – headed by the President of the European association thus allowing only a marginal role to be played by the Brussels secretariats and the affiliated European intermediary associations.

At the second Egmont Palace meeting, taking place on 12 January 1989 – a year and a half after the first dialogue review – a political steering group was set up.[184] This was comprised of bureaucrats from the European associations which for the first time were given a role in the process apart from planning preparatory meetings. Most of the preparatory work is carried out by the CEU which effectively has sponsored the whole arrangement from its own funds. No dedicated dialogue secretariat has been set up by the CEU but the process has been monitored closely be senior officials from both the President's cabinet and the cabinet of the commissioner in charge of DGV.[185]

The second Egmont Palace meeting initiated a new phase of the dialogue which had experienced its first crisis as the partners had been unable to reach agreement on a joint statement on the 1988–89 Annual Economic Report. Work on a more comprehensive joint opinion concerning new technologies, work organisation and adaptability of the labour market was, in addition, not progressing.[186] Furthermore, the struggle over the social charter had awakened and amplified past grievances between the UNICE and ETUC. Finally the original action programme, designed to add substance to the Charter, had caused a breakdown of relations between the Spanish commissioner in charge of DGV, Manual Marin, and the trade union movement.

The first proposal produced by Marin was thus widely considered to be non-committed by trade unionists as it called for the Council to adopt unbinding recommendations rather than directives and regulations.[187] Marin, who was both a socialist and former trade unionist, had chosen this cautious strategy in anticipation of stiff Council opposition should he have proposed more substantial measures. Likewise the coming into effect of the Single European Act in 1987 had caused considerable unease among employer associations as it directly referred to European level agreements between the social partners.[188] Delors solved the deadlock by promoting Marin to commissioner responsible for fisheries policies – a far more important portfolio from a Spanish perspective as they have by far the Union's largest fleet of fishing vessels. His replacement in DGV was Greek socialist Mrs Vasso Papandreous – a passionate supporter of dialogue.

Employers were also offered a token for re-entering dialogue. The CEU offered to consult the social partners on all initiatives taken under the auspices of the Social Action Programme, the European Company Statute and the Regional Aid Programmes.[189] This helped to allude an aura of consultation rather than negotiation to the dialogue setting. By establishing a steering committee, the battle was in fact won by the CEU who by way of this organisational innovation had ensured a larger role would be played by the Brussels secretariats – the employees of which were more naturally prone to EU initiatives in the field than the constituent national associations.

Headed by Mrs Papandreou the steering committee held its first meeting on 21 March 1989 and confirmed the creation of two new working groups: one on education and training and the second on the labour market.[190] By July 1992 four joint opinions had been produced by the first working group. The second group managed to produced one joint opinion within its own field, and afterwards managed to crack the locked situation around the joint opinion on new technology which was finally signed on 10 January 1991. More importantly, however, the secretariats of the three European associations produced a joint statement on 10 July 1990 calling for national implementation of joint opinions through national social dialogue.[191] This is the first fully recorded independent action taken by the secretariats in the course of the Val Duchesse dialogue.

The dialogue reached its peak when, as already pointed out, on

31 October 1991 the social partners submitted a joint statement to the intergovernmental conference preceding the Maastricth Treaty regarding the future role of the social partners in the EU labour market policy making framework. This agreement was later incorporated into the Treaty with some minor modifications.

### 4.2 The Third Phase: Societal Governance through Network Creation and Discourse Formation

In the Val Duchesse talks the EU seems to have found a durable formula for supranational social dialogue. This has been achieved by (1) excluding governments from the setting and focusing on European level participation; (2) ensuring that participants are somewhat equal with regards to analytical resources; and finally (3) by sustaining the dialogue through a series of non-interrelated topical arenas.[192]

Excluding national governments ensures a balance in the networks under construction as no participants have privileged access to dominant national arenas. In addition it ensures coherence in the ranks of the European level social partners. No advantage is gained by deserting common positions around supranational bargaining tables. The exclusion of national governments, however, prevents the setting from achieving a role as forum for European concerted action as the fiscal element in this policy design rests with Council members.

Although the CEU has been busy disassociating itself from the October agreement – giving full credit to the social partners – it did in fact mastermind the entire run up to the signing of the deal in close cooperation with the European secretariats of the social partners.[193] Political support for CEU action in the field was actively offered by France which occasionally took on the role as participant – as with the initial convening of the Val Duchesse talks.

Most Council members regard the dialogue as an alternative – albeit inefficient – setting for producing EU level labour market rules. Others harbour the more modest expectation that a narrow dialogue, comprising only the social partners, could eventually become an efficient setting for consultation by the Council as envisioned by the Maastricht Treaty.

Based on evidence provided by frequently issued policy statements, the very point of the Val Duchesse exercise has been to establish some form of European societal governance system based on a negotiated growth strategy.[194] Yet similar arrangements were being downgraded in the most advanced member states in the same period. Structural change has often been quoted as the reason for this change of policy in Continental and Scandinavian states. As the most advanced Western societies moved to the 'post-fordist' mode of accumulation, regulatory arrangements were adapted thus leading to a replacement of the 'Keynesian welfare state' by the 'Schumpeterian workfare state'.[195]

Member states possessing the least developed economies in the eighties resorted to the type of neo-corporatist concerted action abandoned by the richer countries. Both Ireland, Portugal, Spain and Greece have at some point during the eighties experimented with cooperative growth strategies. France was facing the challenge of having to manage an advanced economy belatedly succumbing to the pressures of globalisation and significant resistance. Under socialist leadership throughout most of the decade, attempts were made to establish a dialogue between the country's fragmented social partners. This was being particularly vigorously pursued by the then French Minister of Finance, Mr Jacques Delors.

Great Britain set the direction for a new approach to societal management relying on the wonders of market forces. Essentially the British merely refined the institutional traits of its national set-up which, in spite of attempts to introduce neo-corporatist concertation by the Labour Governments of the seventies, were naturally prone to a market-led development path.

The structural crises which had beset Western economies since the early seventies proved particularly straining for Europe. This has been attributed to a mode of societal governance which allegedly emphasises consensus formation at the expense of flexibility. Gradually, the Northwest European Continental states dismantled some of the most salient settings of concertation – or at least downplayed their role in the making of national economic policies. This group of countries would include Germany, The Netherlands and Denmark but also countries like Italy and Belgium experienced a retreat from neo-corporatist aspirations.

Not only the Council was divided on the issue. Parts of other EU bodies such as the CEU, the Parliament and the ESC showed resentment towards the development. In the CEU DGII (economic affairs) seemed divided on the issue and DGIII (industrial affairs) and DG IV (competition) appeared downright hostile.[196] Prominent members of the European Parliament and segments of the ESC were also critical of attempts to introduce Euro-corporatism. The EP social committee chairman, Wim van Velzen, publicly pointed to the undesirable effects on the overall democratic balance of the Union likely to be caused by neo-corporatist structures on a European level. He and others feared a decline of the European Parliament even before it had a chance to become a genuine power centre.[197] This worry reflected the findings of mainly pluralist inspired political science literature which had depicted declining roles of legislators throughout Europe as the executive embarked on concerted arrangements with key societal groupings.

Group III – comprising the professions and consumer interests – feared a marginalisation of the ESC should the social dialogue prove successful in generating a pervasive consensus between the social partners. This leaves France, Belgium and Mr Delors, Mrs Papandreous, DGV and the ETUC bureaucracy as main political backers of social dialogue.

In erecting Val Duchesse the main entrepreneur, the CEU and French socialist elites, have assured that the building blocks of dialogue – the social partners – are equipped for the task. A case in point is the virtual sponsoring of ETUC. The dual nature of the dialogue with parallel settings discussing simultaneously tangible labour market issues such as procedures for implementing new technology and macro oriented reflections on overall economic development, ensures that the actors are exposed to one another in relation to issues on different levels, thus making the setting less vulnerable for complete breakdowns.

The marginal social base of the 'constructed' social partner on the side of labour, appeared to have been a minor concern among proponents of the third phase of European social dialogue. The plurality of policy issues under consideration and the parallel quest for meso- and micro-level dialogue inherent in recent legislation on social protection, suggests that the Val Duchesse set-up differs from classical neo-corporatist arrangements on some important accounts. Hierarchical ideals of societal governance featured in both the political economy ideology of the first and second phase, seem less prominent in the third phase. As pluralism assumes state control with core macroeconomic parameters by means of public redistribution policies, neo-corporatism aligns to Keynesian demand-management achieved jointly by the apparatus of state and organised markets. By contrast the Val Duchesse strategy excludes hierarchical control of, for example, trade union rank and file as vital variables of governance. Labour is invited to the negotiation tables not because they exert direct control of the masses and are accorded the right to conclude binding agreements on behalf of employees at large. Rather trade unions are admitted because of their discursive and legitimating capacity. Settings are thus to be constituted as policy networks where societal problems are identified and rectification strategies outlined. Direct lines of command and control between peak settings and individual workers and firms is no longer determining the viability of dialogue as was the case in the seventies. Softer instruments are thus instituted stressing a public social construction of meanings on societal causal effects, public concerns and individual contributions of actors to their solution. Hence the instruments of governance are networks defining and articulating valid discourses informing the action of societal players. This approach is essentially fuelled by themes and logics associated with the money market rationale.

## 5   THE DYNAMICS OF SOCIAL DIALOGUE

In the previous two chapters it is argued that it is essentially political, rather than economic, pressures driving EU's labour market policy agenda. The origins of this political pressure is not the social partners but key players in the CEU and the Council aiming at a strategic reconfiguration of the European political economy. Rather than being the engines of EU labour market policy integration, trade unions and employer associations respond to the growing significance of the area by upgrading their involvement in an arena designed and sponsored by other actors. This is amply observed in relation to social dialogue.

The composition of actors promoting social dialogue has changed since the signing of the Treaty of Rome. At its inception the ESC was not geared particularly towards social issues in a narrow sense. The making of this body was an outcome of a constitutional game whereas the sectoral dialogues were solely a CEU sponsored venture. Initially the Tripartite Conferences relied heavily on impetus from the Council of Europe, but subsequently it was given no further direct support from member states.

In the establishment of the Val Duchesse talks official documents conveyed the image of social pressures directed towards the Council by the social partners, resulting in CEU dialogue initiatives. Besides the first Egmont Palace meeting of 7 May 1987 where the Council Presidency extraordinarily participated,[198] the Val Duchesse and Egmont Palace talks have not included representatives of member states. In case the Council – and the social partners – wanted to upgrade the social dialogue, a stronger show of commitment within the existing framework of the SCE would have been a logical start. The Council, however, at no point managed to devise a system which could convey a mandate to the Presidency which faced the social partners in the SCE. While both Unions and employers created internal discussion structures to define coherent positions in advance of meetings, the Council displayed strong reservations even towards such modest pledges to effective negotiations.[199]

Both sides of industry showed similar lack of commitment as their delegations mainly consisted of organisation bureaucrats.[200] These delegates could in no way match Council and CEU representatives in terms of political weight. None of the social partners at the European level thus possess the authority to conclude binding deals on labour market issues. In addition divergence among constituent associations would make it next to impossible to nationally implement such deals. Finally, no mechanisms exist to handle non-compliance.

The ability of the CEU in successfully creating institutions depends on its political status and strength. The Tripartite Conferences were hampered by successive calls for more participation from member states. Trade unions in particular did not regard the CEU as a useful negotiating partner.[201] This has obviously changed, a fact which is well illustrated by the arrangement of the Val Duchesse meetings. A number of prominent Commissioners, including Jacques Delors and Vasso Papandreous, in conjunction with bureaucrats from the General Secretariat and DGV, considered the establishment of European level societal governance systems a vital component of an overall structural change strategy in which a hierarchy of negotiated settings are to operate. The EU level is to act as a model although it is envisioned that workable national practices are to be maintained. The underlying philosophy behind this policy is shared by other Commissioners and CEU bureaucracies such as DGXII and DGXIII but runs counter to the prevailing economic philosophy of DGIII and DGVI. As the strategy was masterminded by both the General Secretariat and DGV, the CEU has managed to act as a coherent entity in the matter. Although the CEU clearly took the lead in promoting the social dimension agenda on the political arena, other actors played important parts.[202]

Europe's employers initially strongly resisted taking part in a political process bringing about a European level labour market regime. In the wake of the successful adoption of the neo-liberal internal market scheme, and the general change in economic and political discourse up through the eighties, business saw little reason to give concessions to actors representing an ideology already beaten. Later a more strategic approach was pursued. By in particular stressing dialogue as the means to establish a foundation for common European level labour market regulation, organised employers first attempted to avoid binding legislation in the field while hoping the general push for integration in the economic realm would somehow reflect in a deregulation of national labour markets. Or if this is rephrased, employers intended to use Europe as a vehicle of deregulation where a deluded EU labour market policy setting was eventually to substitute national settings in which labour had a strongly entrenched position. The EU's internal market scheme was to be employed in an attempt to counter the labour market rationale within its own realm. This perspective was not actually advanced by employer organisation representatives – who are co-bearers of the labour market rationale – but rather by industry associations such as the European Roundtable of Industrialists and various supplementing informal associations such as the Gyllehammer group led by the Volvo chairman.

From the perspective of employers, national labour market regimes were largely unaffected by the increased application of neo-liberal rhetorics by national political elites. Looked at through less biased lenses, it would appear that the influence of trade unions was eroded by the coming into power of advocates of neo-liberal strategies in North-western Continental member states. However, while labour power in the North was in decline, Greece, Portugal, Spain and Ireland started to experiment with neo-corporatist strategies. Although the political status of trade unions across member states diverges, all national centres have taken a liking for national bargaining in spite of past or recent experiences. Trade unions nonetheless appreciate that the set-backs suffered by neo-corporatist settings in the eighties and early nineties, were due not only to prominence of neo-classical discourse in political life. The changing character of the world economy and the general thrust for globalisation has undermined the key governance instrument associated with traditional neo-corporatism: Keynesian demand management.[203]

Consequently consensus of national trade union centres evolves around a desire to regain macroeconomic control of negotiated settings by extending the policy arena to the supranational level. European level negotiated settings are thus considered a *supplement* to national settings. By pursuing this strategy it is hoped that the neo-corporatist mode of governance, relying on Keynesian remedies, can be prolonged beyond the collapse of the fordist production paradigm. The CEU and European labour does not share a common vision on the future role of dialogue, but has nonetheless joined in an alliance which is highly imbalanced in favour of the former.

In short European dialogue has evolved through three distinct phases featuring respectively a mixture between the state power and the pure market rationale, the labour market rationale, and finally, the money market rationale. Sponsoring actors have formed different coalitions. The first phase was initially cast by state bodies negotiating the Treaty of Rome. The CEU carried the load both in the latter part of the first phase and throughout most of the second phase. In the third phase the CEU has been acting under French tutelage. In the final chapter the role of EU organisations, states and contending rationales in the shaping of European labour market policy – drawing on the cases investigated in the previous two chapters – will be elaborated further.

# 5 Conclusion: The Dynamics of European Labour Market Integration

## 1 INTRODUCTION

European labour market policy impinges on one of the four freedoms constituting the backbone of the common market. It was politically amputated as a policy field following a row between, chiefly, France and Germany in the constitutional process preceding the signing of the Treaty of Rome.

Yet the EU was equipped with fairly autonomous bodies which have continuously struggled to enhance the legitimacy and state-like appearance of the Union. Neo-functionalism provided the manual for integration strategies. Neo-functionalism assigned co-option of interest groups as the key role in the dynamics of regional integration.

The political economies of the member states are neither designed nor interpreted in accordance with the pluralist ideals implied in neo-functionalism. Hence a hierarchy of interest groups is identified, with core peak organisations representing labour and capital, enjoying privileged access to state sponsored policy arenas. The ideology of integration lends heavily from contemporary American political science, the findings and statements of which was, obviously, contextual in validity. It matched poorly the neo-corporatist, clientalist and 'etatist' realities of post-war Europe.

Hence, in excluding labour market policy as a core Treaty obligation, while instituting mechanisms relying on interaction between the newly formed Euro-polity and interests groups as vehicles of integration, the founding states had created an inherently unstable arrangement. EU bodies, particularly the CEU, were embodied with an immanent aspiration to achieving state-like attributes. In denying the CEU access to the zenith of contemporary statehood – economic management prerogatives – while nurturing the body's elevation of an inadequate policy manual – neo-functionalism – to semi-official

134

ideology, the realm of EU labour market policy was bound to be characterised by rudimentary policy designs, inconsistent tactics and, at best, piecemeal progress.

According to Holloway, EU labour market policy has been beset by an on-going struggle between two opposing camps representing respectively the 'economist' and the 'social-progress' perspective.[204] Proponents of the 'economist' stance have argued that beyond special provisions for migrant workers, the EU should avoid commitments in the realm of social and labour market policy which could be handled more efficiently by means of market mechanisms. By contrast advocates of the 'social-progress' view regard the EU as a tool for redistribution both between member states and between social strata within individual countries. Following Holloway the 'economist' camp won the battle in the wake of the 1967 show-down between the CEU – originally opting for the 'social-progress' line – and member states wary of interference.

This study suggests that no final victory has been achieved by either of the sides in that the social dimension to the internal market contains elements pointing to the 'social-progress' view written off by Holloway in 1981. Findings also indicate that a third camp has a stake in debates on European labour market policy. They side with adherents to the 'social-progress' perspective in pledging commitments to an integrated Europe going beyond free flows of goods, services and factors of production. Unlike backers of the 'social-progress' line, however, the third stance consider labour markets and associated policies mainly as tools of societal governance rather than instruments dedicated to the improvement of living conditions for workers.[205]

The social dialogue is commonly considered merely an attachment to the social dimension. Historically, EU labour market policy has moved from concrete regulation – enacted to assist the factor market system in operating as efficiently as possible – to the present situation were proponents of EU activity in the area attempt to establish a framework of societal governance resting on customised institutions. Accordingly, policy proposals have been insubstantial and in addition only implementable if widespread derogations are allowed as national schemes already in operation – usually providing far broader coverage – vary tremendously and can in no way be substituted by the meagre directives diluted and subsequently passed by the Council.

This suggests that establishing a framework of societal governance assumes higher priority at the present stage, among chief proponents of Social Europe, than the making of substantial policies. The CEU has taken on a very dominant role in forming policy networks which are to evolve into overall frameworks for a European socio-economic governance system. This network formation process has been approached partly by granting privileged access to certain actors and partly by means of a funding scheme which has in effect balanced the protagonist entities whenever the distribution of power resources seemed too unequal. A case in point is the establishment – with EU funding – of the Trade Union Technical Bureau in connection with the making of health and safety policies. The very establishment of policy networks thus seems to be a key motive behind the enterprising participation of the CEU in promoting the creation of a European societal governance system. Directives in the labour market field are to be interpreted as merely baits for the social partners which previously has had few incentives to devote time and resources to the European level. Hence the dynamics of European labour market policy integration places dialogue above legislation and is underpinned by political rather than economical forces.

Judged by the rhetorics of senior CEU officials and Mrs Papandreous, the aspiration of key EU policy makers is to create a European societal governance system founded on a German inspired political economy. France particularly strives to recast its present system and use the EU as a vehicle for that purpose. The CEU's commitment has been fuelled by the desire to create a truly common market based on a joint institutional framework. DGV has thus repeatedly expressed its wish to nurture a 'European mode of production' allegedly based on North-west Continental European experiences.[206]

This project is to be seen as a counter initiative to the attempts at stylising the Continental economies according to the British model. Besides traditional political action within the framework of the Union's constitutional system, the CEU relentlessly stresses the enhancement of dialogue. This is supported by frequent references to the term 'a negotiated growth strategy' by Vasso Papandreous, Jacques Delors and French government officials in 'Social Europe', the special publication labelled 'Joint Opinions' and official statements as conveyed by the mass media.

In policies of social protection the issue seems to be the erection of micro- and meso-level patterns of dialogue devoid of the antagonist spirit characteristic of industrial relations informed mainly by the labour market rationale. Likewise the emphasis on 'partnership' at the macro-level suggests that while pure market ideals are considered inappropriate for labour markets, traditional antagonism is not a worthy substitute.

The CEU's policy preferences as expressed by Mr Delors and Mrs Papandreous, contain elements of a labour market rationale. Yet they also incorporate properties of the money market rationale. They are definitely in opposition to the pure market rationale and also reflects ideological fatigue vis-à-vis the state power rationale which incidentally is harboured by the crisis-prone political economies of both France and Greece. Yet employing the labour market in a societal governance strategy is not incompatible with either a state power or a pure market rationale. All four identified rationales may thus accommodate societal governance strategies involving labour markets.

Historically this is most clearly reflected in the development of the macro-level social dialogue as it has progressed (or degenerated) through three distinct phases combining unique mixes of the four rationales. To some extent this also applies to the field of social protection. The first phase of social dialogue was thus paired by EU social legislation on the packaging and labelling of dangerous substances – in effect creating a common market for production inputs disguised as labour protection. The second phase in the realm of legislation emphasised the granting of rights to particular groups. Equal opportunity thus received substantial attention and certain rights were granted to workers in general in relation to firm closures and take-overs. But the main battle-ground emerged over the issue of worker representation in management. In the third phase, legislation – as already pointed out – seems to stress institution building.

In the following the three strategies of societal governance, reflected in the three distinct phases of EU social policy, will be subject to closer scrutiny. The underlying rationales will be identified and future prospects for labour market integration will be discussed in the closing section.

## 2  STRATEGIES OF SOCIETAL GOVERNANCE

The EU's attempts of employing the labour market sphere in the conduct of societal governance, has grouped around three distinct strategies. The first strategy is marked by an optimistic view of the capacity of the political sphere in manipulating markets. The second strategy rests on the intellectual pillars of neo-corporatism, attempts are made to organise markets and co-opted by the state sphere. In the third strategy policy makers are increasingly abandoning formal political regulation of the market and are instead, following the experiments of unleashed economic anarchy of the eighties, resorting to soft, long-term steering instruments aiming at manipulating the most fundamental and the most inaccessible variable of government: how we think politics. Creation of meaning – essentially a civil society task – hence becomes the object of government.

## 2.1   Societal Governance through State Intervention: Strategy I

The first phase of social dialogue and social protection policies was strongly affected by the fact that the Union was at an early stage of development. Hence no firmly established institutions could be employed in the advance of new institutions.

Likewise the composition of actors reflected that European level politics initially was in the realm of central state bodies such as foreign ministries. Yet these bodies could be subjected to rationales of other spheres successfully colonising the institutions of statehood.

The devastating effects of war had, however, extended beyond material damage. In Germany there was a political atmosphere of purification – amply displayed in the 'stunde null' metaphor – fuelling an apparent purge of previous institutional preferences harboured by state and market actors. While continuity can easily be observed between pre-nazi era and post-war institutional designs, they were more or less concealed in liberalist jargon in the years immediately following the creation of the federal republic.

In particular the state bodies entrusted with foreign affairs – conducting the delicate relations with the former occupying powers – were eager to pledge allegiance to the liberal state image. Hence in early negotiations Germany, today identified with the 'social market economy', became advocates of the pure market rationale. It was thus German negotiators who objected to French concerns of social dumping.

France, another traditional proponent of the liberal state ideal, was on the other hand concerned with resurrecting the authority of a state apparatus badly bruised by the humiliating defeat in both the Second World War and various subsequent colonial campaigns. Although both countries adhered to the liberal state ideal, Germany was more biased towards the 'liberal' dimension whereas France stressed the 'state' dimension.

Italy, traditionally preoccupied with instituting state authority –

although often in vain – had also suffered defeat in the war. This did not produce the overall dismantling of societal governance structures as in Germany. Yet the country was eager to demonstrate commitment to both international trade and responsible European state cooperation.

The Benelux countries had shown the way forward with their internal customs union. None of these smaller states had suffered the severe blows to established structures as the three larger founding members. In recognition of their limited political weight, they adopted highly constructive and pragmatic positions. The institutional balance at the creation of the EU thus stood between a state power and a pure market rationale.

Both the set-up of the ESC and the initiation of the sectoral dialogues are to be interpreted in the light of the attempts of creating a European polity. Labour market policy objectives were vague and the major concern seemed to be adding some muscle and legitimacy to the newly formed supranational entity – a strategy obviously informed by state power ideals.

Theoretically the legacy of neo-functionalism, with its implicit application of pluralist democratic theory, is evident. Although access to a number of settings were granted by the Council and the CEU, a basic belief in competition is reflected in the heterogeneity of actors admitted to the ESC. The sectoral dialogues appear somewhat more neo-corporatist at first glance. However, the initiation of sectoral arenas with no co-ordinating superstructure gives evidence of a prevailing theoretical outlook featuring classic pluralist segmentation.

The high level of detail in early proposals for health and safety regulation (stipulating the social rights of migrant labour) and the dominant legal approach to equal opportunity, point to a 'dirigist' path which, while in variance with traditional pluralism, suggests a common understanding of societal governance among the constituent entities featuring potent governing capacity of central power structures be they national or supranational. Political science and political economy of this first strategy for European labour market policy was thus based on common intellectual ground reflected in the perception of the state and the market.

Pluralist democratic theory offers a coherent description of the workings of western type political systems albeit with a heavy bias towards competitive polities like the ones operating in the USA and the UK. Most contemporary work on the institutional shaping of markets took the role of the state as the point of departure. The relative economic decline of the United Kingdom in comparison with its main competitors on world markets, was the empirical starting point of much early research in the field. A 'societal engineering' approach dominates the literature up through the sixties and seventies. Setting up the 'right' institutions would thus ensure any country or region, regardless of the character of the dominant societal mode, a desired growth regime.

Shonfield's analysis of the role of the French state in boosting economic performances way beyond what had been achieved by Britain, was a symptomatic reflection of the contemporary focus of academia and policy makers towards the blessings of a 'dirigist' approach to economic planning.

The emphasis on the blessings of state intervention is intrinsically linked to the belief that markets are fairly easy targets for manipulation. By redirecting investment flows and generating demands, the marked behaviour of previously singled out agents, be they industries or consumers, could be altered in a desirable direction.

Theories of policy making featuring an image of the distributional (weak) or programmatic (strong) state subject to external pressure from interest groups could easily be accommodated to the findings of political economy since pluralists regarded the state as central to all political calculation and political economists portrayed the state as the central institution of market economies. The view of the nature of markets was thus closely aligned with the prevalent view of politics in the fifties, sixties and early seventies. These 'modern' ideals were consequently adopted and served as inputs in the nurturing of European level ideals on societal governance by particularly the CEU. Eventually it was the market aspect of the liberal state ideal which prevailed as the sponsoring state – Germany – exhibits considerably more diachronic coherence than that of France.

### 2.2   Societal Governance through Co-option of Organised Markets: Strategy II

As memories of war faded among political, administrative and business elites, the institutional convergence, which had fuelled integration in the first place, was bound to contact difficulties as states re-entered previous institutional paths. As war fundamentally threatens national markets and states, the state sphere – controlling the instruments which might ensure national survival – is bound to achieve relative hegemony while hostilities abound. Yet as peace re-surfaces contending spheres will re-emerge from submission eager to establish a previous or a new institutional equilibrium.

Europe's honeymoon ended as the first oil crisis sparked off recession. In the meantime Germany – and partly Denmark and The Netherlands – had relinquished itself from the pure market ideal and vigorously preached the gospel of the social market economy. The labour market rationale had assumed relative hegemony. The consequent strategy of concerted action was widely accredited for providing a rather smooth German passage through world recession.

Other countries, most notably Britain, attempted to imitate central features of the neo-corporatist crisis management model. It quickly proved incompatible with the historically evolved institutional configuration framing this country's industrial relations. Trade union coherence was constantly challenged by independent minded shop stewards and relations between the Labour Party governments and trade union leadership seemed to rest as much on internal competition as unified rallying around the common course so essential to the labour market rationale.

Also France and Italy were seeking inspiration from the German brand of neo-corporatism as a means of enhancing their crisis management capabilities. The problems facing these two political economies were, however, as different as one can possible imagine. Italy was crippled by inadequate state powers whereas France suffered from a situation of 'institutional crowding out', as the state levied such pervasive powers on all aspects of the country's growth and governance regime.

In France efforts to accommodate labour in national deals took a different turn than in Britain and Germany. While the latter country could rely on a complex system of bargaining placing the export-oriented metal and chemical sectors as national pace-setters, Britain sought to please wary labour by ill-fated Keynesian policies which eventually only strained the national budget while fuelling discontent among greedy shop stewards. The French state, however, attempted to cater for perceived labour demands by increasingly sealing off the country from foreign competition by a notorious system of non-tariff barriers.

Hence recession in the seventies sparked off a realignment in Europe's main political economies as labour – and the labour market rationale – was increasingly enlisted in pursuit of national crisis management strategies. As conditions for labour participation varied tremendously between EU member countries, policy outcomes fundamentally diverged. The German model was ultimately successful in saving the country from massive de-industrialisation, but critics would argue that this was achieved at a high democratic toll. The French approach seriously disrupted trade and threatened to drag the continent into a downward spiral of beggar-my-neighbour policies. Britain's policies led to near economic collapse and social unrest and hence posed a challenge to stability. European level responses thus chiefly aimed at aligning incompatible national political economic strategies.

The efforts of the second strategy is best understood as an attempt of extending succesful neo-corporatist practices of certain member states to the supranational level. The agenda, aim and design of the setting clearly reflects the neo-corporatist aspirations. These aspirations are expressed mainly in connection with the social dialogue as this type of arrangement traditionally has been associated with the making of grand policy designs rather than tangible issues such as equal opportunity and health and safety. Correspondingly the dominant items on the social protection agenda of the seventies concerned the extension of rights to collective entities, rather than products or individual migrant workers, as during the first phase.

As stated in chapter 4, most North-western European countries, starting in the inter-war period, witnessed a continuous dialogue between government and the social partners. This dialogue found its most vivid expression in the frameworks for concerted action denoting institutionalised bargaining between labour, capital and state in which the former moderates its short term demands in exchange for long-run concessions with regards to job creation and influence on macroeconomic policy making.

A central element of neo-corporatist practices is the process of consensus-formation in which the prevailing understanding of the nature of the common good guide decision making. Politically generating broad elite consensus on broad policy themes requires micro-level institutions highlighting trust and reciprocity. The mix of rationales with which labour form the overall national political economic institutional configuration thus condition the scope for macro-level governance strategy. Hence neo-corporatism as practised in Germany relies as much on the post-war legacy of the money market rationale as the prominence given to labour from the late sixties and onwards. Although the labour market rationale successfully challenged the state and product market rationales of France and Britain in the seventies, imitation of the German mode of governance was not necessarily feasible.

At the European level, refuge was nonetheless taken in the only operating national system displaying some success in both countering crises and enrolling labour. Hence attempts were made to transplant the overall governance framework of Germany to the European level. This obviously proved a highly frustrating exercise as fragmented elite preferences of crises-prone national systems were aggregated and hence amplified at the Brussels arena. The appeal of neo-corporatism eroded as results failed to materialise in political economies which had previously displayed strongly state or market centred systems. A general failure to appreciate the importance of micro-level institutions and a political inability to alter them, served to discredit the merits of negotiated societal management while in addition dwarfing the labour market rationale as dramatically illustrated by the policies subsequently adopted by the United Kingdom under Mrs Thatcher.

### 2.3 Societal Governance through Network Creation and Discourse Formation: Strategy III

In the Val Duchesse talks governments are excluded from the setting which focus on European level participation. The CEU has ensured that participants are somewhat equal with regard to analytical resources and dialogue is sustaining through a series of non-interrelated topical arenas. The nurturing of micro-level – dialogue prone – institutions is embedded in both the health and safety and the maternity directives.

The inability of Keynesian macroeconomics to cope with Western Europe's structural crises sparked off a quest for flexibility resulting in the apparent dismantling of neo-corporatist institutions.

While most continental governments down-played their commitment to national negotiation, major European countries with comparative levels of economic development and highly integrated through the EU, persisted in performing differently on global markets in spite of the apparent convergence in government-industry relations, finance-industry relations and last but not least industrial relations at large.

This has been attributed to differences in the societal foundations of macro socio-political institutions across Europe. Academics – such as David Soskice – increasingly draw attention to the operation of 'institutional infrastructures' and 'social learning mechanisms' which predispose individual societies towards specific governance and policy strategies.[207] Soskice thus points to the duration of, and level of trust in, relations between societal actors and the state as being particularly important in shaping the general political environment.

The preoccupation with meso- and micro-structures such as networks and institutional infrastructures in political science and economics alike, signifies, as pointed out by Wolfgang Streeck, a general shift in outlook with regard to societal governance away from the macro-level.[208] Likewise Patrick Kenis and Volker Schneider[209] contend that with the advent of the policy network terminology the focus of societal governance has moved from hierarchical control systems to horizontal co-ordination. This corresponds with the findings of both the negotiated economy approach and David Soskice.

A third image of the political economy, frequently pointing to Germany and Scandinavia as model cases, has seemingly gained a foothold on the Brussels agenda. It is perhaps best summarised as the negotiated approach, as it moves the locus of inquiry away from the apparatus of state towards socio-institutional actors. The latter's role in the conduct of national economic management is assessed stressing measures enhancing non-opportunistic behaviour.

Social dialogue is by its very nature an attempt of arranging the policy universe in a particular manner giving high priority to the supranational level of the social partners. Given the weakness of the particular EU bodies supposed to resemble the state in national systems, the *raison d'être* of a negotiated regime is mainly to infuse a feeling of community (Gemeinschaft) among the regions corporate and trade union elites. This is done by nurturing long-term and stable relationships displaying a high degree of mutual trust between the social partners.

These macro-level initiatives are supplemented by similarly aimed trust enhancing schemes implanted in legislation on social protection. In sum, the increased awareness of the micro aspects of labour market operations bears witness to a shift away from the collectivity centred labour market rationale towards the more relational money market rationale.

## 2.4   Societal Governance: Between Hierarchical Control and Horizontal Coordination

The EU's engagement in labour market policy has intellectually clustered around three coherent conceptual logics – or strategies. The first strategy is marked by an optimistic view of the capacity of the political sphere in manipulating the market. The second strategy is associated with the era of neo-corporatism, markets were sought organised and employed in the conduct of government.

As the process of industrialisation gained momentum in the wake of the Second World War, the dominant mode of societal management in Western Europe relied on horizontal control mechanisms resting either on the state or the involvement in the conduct of government by peak interest groupings representing both sides of industry. Strategy one and two thus prevailed in key countries such as France and Germany respectively. While this has reflected in some ambiguity as regards the societal governance strategy for the EU at large, consensus established at the creation of the Union, narrowed the scope of conflict regarding governance strategy on the two opposing approaches to horizontal steering staged by strategy one and two.

During the late seventies and eighties emphasis of theoretically founded work on societal governance has, moved from a top-down towards a bottom-up perspective. As the process of globalisation prompted governments to dismantle – or down-grade – the high salience neo-corporatist institutional structures constituting the defining traits of the continental European fordist growth path, political economists focused their attention on micro-founded 'institutional infrastructures' when accounting for persistent variance in economic performance by countries possessing comparable factor endowments and experiencing a convergence in the macro-institutional configuration of their economies. Following the third strategy, policy makers are increasingly abandoning formal political regulation of the market and are instead following the experiments of the unleashed economic anarchy of the eighties, resorting to soft, long-term steering instruments aiming at manipulating the most fundamental and the most inaccessible variable of government: how we think politics.

Table 3 summarises the three strategies of societal governance. Denoting the various modes of societal governance 'strategies' implies that policy makers are facing a situation where they can pick one instead of the other at their own discretion. However, as should be evident from the preceding discussion, a given strategy is dependent on institutions which in turn are historically rooted and culturally embedded. An important element of this 'embeddedness' is the 'institutional infrastructures' identified by Soskice. Societies are thus biased towards one or two of the strategies due to their specific institutional configuration. Policy makers are consequently not entering an open playing field when determining which strategy to follow.

146 *The Political Economy of a Social Europe*

Strategy two is clearly the most demanding of the three with regard to the efficiency of formal institutions such as the government bureaucracy and the social partners. It in addition requires some specific features of the institutional infrastructures which cannot easily be recreated at the European level.

*Table 3*

| Strategies of societal governance | Societal governance through state intervention | Societal governance through co-option of organised markets | Societal governance through network creation and discourse formation |
|---|---|---|---|
| **Political science approach** | Pluralist-democratic theory | Neo-corporatism | New-institutionalism, neo-pluralism (policy networks) |
| **Economic approach** | Macroeconomics: markets are competitive and subject to political manipulation | Macroeconomics: markets are organised, peak organisations are bearers of political authority | Institutional economics, micro-oriented: markets embedded in social institutions |
| **Political focus (Unit of analysis)** | Selfish political *actors* struggling over distributional outcomes | Hierarchical system of bargaining *structures* | Networks, formal and informal *institutions* |
| **Policy instruments for economic management** | State intervention – the state is central to all political calculations | Macro-level consensus formation | Network creation and discourse formation |
| **Character of policy outcomes** | Short–medium term distributional | Medium–long term distributional | Softly programmatic |
| **Weaknesses** | Complexity of markets outweigh states' political capacity for intervention | Factor market rigidity and consequent pressures for flexibility | Great uncertainty as processes evolve over the long run with a multiplicity of actors |

Governance strategies align to rationales. Strategy I is associated to both the state power and the pure market rationale. Strategy II finds its expression in the labour market rationale and finally Strategy III is best accommodated within the money market rationale. The relative position of rationales determine the choice of strategy while institutional micro-features determine the applicability of a given strategy. Britain may thus adopt strategy III if the City musters the required political power to successfully institute the money market rationale in Whitehall. Yet, given the institutional configuration of the country it may prove difficult to implement.

## 3 STATES, MARKETS, STRATEGIES AND RATIONALES

In the context of the EU at large, national political struggles, in an interplay with European level processes, determine the choice of strategy. States experience varying degrees of centralisation and societal integration. States institutionalise political power which may originate from the apparatus of states themselves or from central market actors including participants in the labour, money and product markets.

When looking at the attitudes of individual states towards both the social dimension in general and the social dialogue in particular, it seems that on no previous occasion has a policy, which at the same time could potentially expand the scope of the Union and change the very nature of economic and labour market policy making at the European level, been initiated with such timid Council backing.

The Val Duchesse dialogue expands over a decade. At early Council sessions, when calls were made for an intensification of the near extinct dialogue of the Tripartite Conferences, the issue was considered non-contagious. The very nature of social dialogue relinquished the Council of having to act on the vast majority of potential outcomes. Thus when confronted with the issue of dialogue, both in connection with the drawing up of the Single European Act and the Maastricht Treaty, heads of states and governments reacted favourably. Past experience suggested the social dialogue constituted an inexpensive component, both politically and economically, of European labour market integration.

France and Belgium appear to be the most enthusiastic supporters of both European labour market policies at large and social dialogue. Italy strongly favoured labour regulation and could at the most muster lukewarm support for the dialogue process. Germany and The Netherlands were moderate supporters of labour regulation but were very concerned about the political cohesion of the Union. Both states invested substantial efforts in avoiding a complete isolation of the strongest opponent to social Europe: Great Britain. Besides Britain, Denmark throughout most of the eighties expressed some reservations towards both projects on grounds of concern about diminishing flexibility.

The internal market scheme aligns itself to the prevalent economic thinking of the eighties epitomised by Margaret Thatcher of the United Kingdom. It was devised on the basis of a particular economic institutional setting found in Anglo-Saxon countries operating what has been termed a company-led growth regime – which in turn falls within the framework of strategy I. In the company-led path, government has an arms-length approach to industry, labour markets are competitive with weak trade unions and the financial system relies on capital markets to cater for the needs of private industry making business geared to short-term profit generation causing a high frequency of bankruptcies and hostile take-overs. Essentially the company-led growth regime – and strategy I – exhibits all the virtues of the pure market rationale.

Unleashed market powers can in itself bring about substantial institutional changes in member countries. Achieving a genuine internal market without an accompanying growth regime informed by a pure market rationale, requires the creation of appropriate institutional mechanisms on the supranational level keeping undesired institutional deterioration in check. The social dimension is such a check and hence detrimental to UK state interests.

Spain voiced concern regarding the costs to the Mediterranean countries of introducing higher social standards at a critical moment of their economic development. The two other poor Mediterranean member states seem not officially to have adopted views similar to the Spanish position, but it appears a valid proposition that similar concerns were clutched in Athens, Lisbon and perhaps even Dublin.[210] Separating general views on the charter and the dialogue respectively for this group of countries, is difficult as their overall position on both issues were ambiguous. To the extent they wanted to avoid binding regulations undermining their competitive position vis-à-vis the Northern member states, they had good reason to display enthusiasm for a negotiated approach relying on the European social partners.

At the same time some scepticism towards actually having social partners producing labour market regulation was voiced domestically in connection with national attempts of concertation as, in particular, trade unions only organised a marginal proportion of the labour force. The issue of *'erga omnis'* – referring to the question of the inclusion of non-organised labour in centrally concluded accords on labour market regulation between social partners – prompted southern actors to look to the Belgian model for a system which simultaneously ensured binding enforceable regulation to be produced and a central consensus formation function to be performed. The Belgian system of national bargaining passes deals concluded between social partners on to Parliament which more or less automatically converts them into law.

Conclusion 149

Italy would be somewhat critical of dialogue while strongly support-
ing EU labour regulation. Issues like *'erga omnis'* and the historical
inability of extending the system of industrial relations practised in
the North to the corrupt and impoverished South, partly explain the
position taken. The emergence of Third Italy – comprising the
regions Emile-Romanie, Umbria, Tuscany and Lazio – as powerful
economic centres may have also affected the country's shaky position
on social dialogue. This part of the country effectively constituted an
economic system on its own relying on informal regulation, flexibility
and network creation rather than the rigid neo-corporatist model
found in the 'fordist' North. Third Italy was hailed by prominent
scholars as constituting the institutional set-up of the future – a model
case of a post-fordist economy having transgressed into the regions
institutional configuration.[211]
  The much celebrated Paris-Bonn axis were largely in accord on the
issue of dialogue. Being aware of French enthusiasm for developing a
social aspect to European integration and the ferocity of British resistance, the Germans could have chosen to take on the role as an
intermediary or buffer between French and UK Council representatives. Germany's political economy is fundamentally attuned with the
agenda advanced by the French. Since Brandt introduced the notion
of a Community with 'a human face' in the early seventies, Germany
has displayed more hesitancy on EU labour market policy. The
change of government in the early eighties accounts for the change of
style, but the down tuning of 'Social Europe' in the country's EU
profile was undoubtedly also affected by the domestic deterioration
of labour power as the money market rationale triumphed following
the making of the ERM. The French agenda sought to combine
labour issues with the money market rationale. Hence Germany saw
it fit to back France in the struggle against the awkward Islanders.
This backing could prove crucial for future developments. While the
French provided a fully-fledged and coherent real-time drive for the
agenda, Germany provided a somewhat more passive shield of
consent. As the diachronic incoherence of the French state permeates
resulting in faltering drive behind the social dimension, Germany's
capacity for long-term political leverage in the field will be greatly
assisted by the compatibility of the policy aim with the country's
currently operating political economy – strongly embedded in institutions of civil society.
  Formal and informal bodies acting within the supranational framework of the EU assumed an important role in maintaining and

expanding the labour market agenda. While relatively autonomous, the CEU has relied on intimate French cooperation in order to advance the policies of the Charter and the dialogue. Yet implementing DGV's aspirations to nurture a 'European mode of production' based on North-west Continental European experiences is a highly complicated task which raises a wide set of questions regarding the macro-political capacity for effectuating micro-level economic change. Apparently a strategy has been devised which leaves it for the supranational level to nurture a political climate which makes national systems predisposed to the negotiated option. As the successful operation of such a system is dependent on culturally embedded institutionally infrastructures, the frameworks attempted for the negotiated approach is likely to evolve towards a system based on network creation and discourse formation rather than traditional neo-corporatist consensus formation. As the CEU is approaching its institution building strategy at both the macro, meso and micro level as expressed in the three cases, it seems that the macro-centred strategy of the seventies has been abandoned in recognition of the political-cultural heterogeneity of Europe.

The CEU departments sponsoring a Social Europe have hosted three different rationales – and labour market policy strategies – in the span of the EU's existence. EU labour market policy has comprised components of both social protection and societal governance. With the social dimension following the SEM, dialogue – the societal governance component – assumed supremacy at the expense of social protection. Social protection policies are increasingly, as demonstrated in chapter 3, devised in a manner ensuring micro-level institutional support to dialogue strategies. Protectional substance is sacrificed in order to acquire stable patterns of labour–capital relations. EU labour market policy is thus informed by the money market rather than the labour market rationale. The European Parliament appreciates the micro- and meso-level dialogue components of EU legislation but has natural reservations towards the Val Duchesse dialogue. Institutional competition places the European Parliament in an awkward position as it has traditionally adopted a radical pro-social dimension stance. Yet the wider implications of the publicly stated strategy threatens to marginalise the body in future policy processes.

In sum, the policy landscape is fragmented as different states and formal EU bodies all support some elements of the 'Social Europe' package put forward by the CEU and France. Basic socio-institutional compatibility ensures timid support from a number of advanced economies. It is the dialogue process which assumes highest priority in project 'Social Europe'. Legislation is advanced mainly to promote dialogue at other levels according to uniform patterns across the Union and in order to make the EU labour market policy arena substantial enough to ensure the involvement of the social partners.

Project 'social dimension' is to be viewed as a counter initiative to the attempts of stylising the Continental economies according to the British model as inherent in the project '1992' design. In pursuit of this aim, the CEU is essentially opting for a strategy of expanded elite socialisation! As such, little has changed since the heyday of neo-functionalism. But while elite socialisation in the sixties was considered an appendix which could enhance the effect of economic spillover processes, the changing character of the global economic system has made 'discourse formation' and the nurturing of consensual modes of policy making one of the few instruments available when politically attempting to bring about a transformation of national and regional economic structures.

## 4 PROSPECTS FOR THE FUTURE

As stated in chapter 2, integration is instigated in anticipation of welfare gains. Yet the positive effects of increased intra-industry trade may be countered by welfare losses suffered by individuals, firms or regions due to increased inter-industry trade. Lacking redistributive measures countering pure market allocation effects of integration, is set to cause alarming disparities between regions and citizens turning them into either winners or losers severely erodes public support and legitimacy. At the macro-level structural policies may be devised to alleviate dislocated regions while social policy seeks to cater for dislocated segments of the workforce.

An alternative perspective stressing market making and societal governance has been outlined by the present study. Accordingly the labour market has been presented as a key component of the overall political economic system. Controlling it politically decisively enhanced the governance capacity of central authorities. This aspect has been dealt with in the preceding analysis under the heading 'societal governance'. Yet, in addition, the institutional feature of labour markets fundamentally affects the ability of our economies to generate growth and cope with the challenges of structural change. The

European Union essentially seeks to integrate markets. The success criterion for this endeavour is growing cross-border transactions. The instruments, however, relate to the configuration of institutions shaping market operations – and consequently dynamics.

Regional integration is market integration. Some markets are integrated to enhance cross-border transactions – such as most consumer and capital goods – while others need to be subjected to a uniform regime because they severely affect the prospects of creating dynamics effects in other markets subject to amalgamation. Hence labour market integration may be seen as carried forth not by a desire to increase cross-border labour flows, but rather to ensure genuine integration of dependent markets redefined by the free flow of goods and capital. A truly single European Market needs a common labour regime as much as a common money regime.

Just like lacking a money dimension is likely to produce local capital bottlenecks, inefficiencies and disequilibrium, a heterogeneous labour regime could pervert the regional allocation of capital, undermine efforts to link national manufacturing systems in comprehensive user-producer networks, and perhaps most important, establish Trans-European business units conducive for synergetic effects.

Accordingly, at least two scenarios can be identified in relation to the future prospects of the social dimension. The most elaborate of these boasts a fully-fledged European welfare system, comprised of social and labour market policy, aiming at securing the welfare of individual citizens and society by means of *redistribution* policies.

The second scenario points to the erection of an overall labour market regime as the desirable and only attainable outcome of the social dimension. A labour market regime defines the overall system of labour market management – or the overall mode of regulation. The regime thus identifies the actors at various levels and sets the basic norms and practices applied in the process of regulation. In essence a joint labour market regime endeavours to install a common institutional order framing labour market operations throughout the EU. In effect this scenario stresses the *market integration* dimension of European level action in the field.

### 4.1   Euro-Wide Redistribution

On the basis of the redistribution dimension, two imperatives behind the launching of the Social Charter are commonly identified. They rest on concerns for the allocation effects of capital and product market integration on the one hand and the lacking popular legitimacy of the European venture on the other.

A widespread fear among trade unionists prevailed on the subject of social dumping following the adoption of the Single European Market scheme. The free movement of capital and goods were thus to result in pressures on member states with highly developed systems for labour protection. Northern countries were to abandon welfare schemes in favour of more *laissez-faire* minded policies in order to gain competitive advantages vis-à-vis low cost Mediterranean countries. French concerns revealed at initial EEC treaty negotiations in relation to equal treatment essentially adhered to the social dumping argument – but chiefly this perspective has been associated with trade unions supposedly exerting societal pressure for EU labour market policy.

The social dumping thesis has particularly been forwarded by German trade union officials. German labour enjoys a high level of legal protection and comprehensive welfare systems dealing with pensions, health and redundancy. This induces costs on employers as they contribute to the abovementioned schemes while at the same time suffer under regulatory constraints.

Cross-national differences in employer contributions to social schemes make up the bulk of variations in overall labour costs. Provisions regulating health and safety standards, employment protection and equality between men and women also has a real impact on the overall level of production costs. The social dumping thesis consequently predicts that in an internal market, companies will settle in regions with modest schemes for social contributions and lower standards for general employment conditions. Competition between regions in attracting investment may henceforth lead to a lowering of standards in the more prosperous areas.

Thus two propositions make up the social dumping argument. The first asserts that labour costs in a wide sense determine the geographical allocation of business investments. The second string of the argument holds that competitive pressure will result in a lowering of national standards for working conditions.[212]

Regardless of the controversy of the social dumping thesis it was the prime *official* motivation for the Social Charter and the associated action programme in the late eighties. Since the early nineties CEU officials have distanced themselves from the social dumping thesis. New discourses in business economics and location theory point to the importance of factors other than cost in determining the international competitiveness of regions and countries. Infrastructure and labour force skills are broadly viewed as the determents for 'higher-order' competitiveness as it has been phrased by Michael Porter.[213] It is thus widely appreciated, even in the Directorate-General responsible for social affairs, that differences in productivity equal out differences in total labour costs.[214]

Winning support for the internal market scheme has been cited as the second prime motive for initiating the Social Dimension. Anticipated problems with trade unions due to perceived adverse distributional effects of the internal market, may have prompted the CEU and key member states to devise a social policy path giving promises of future rewards for labour showing patience with short-term setbacks.

Allocation concerns in the wake of market integration will persist to provide inputs to the policy agenda regardless of the theoretical credentials of the social dumping thesis. However, a number of factors are likely to inhibit it from gaining a firm foothold on European level.

For once, purely technical – or practical – barriers relate to the trivial, albeit extremely important, fact that European welfare systems work mainly through transfers. Although the EU is engaged in transferring funds for social purposes, these are directed at regions rather than individuals. In addition, given the modest proportion of Community fiscal resources compared with the continent's combined GDP, it seems unlikely that the EU is to become a major provider of funds for social transfers or social institutional operating costs.

Redistribution as a prime EU social policy objective finds institutional shelter within the realm of the labour market and the state power sphere. Initiating policies to reward a disadvantaged party still possessing sufficient political muscle to upset the *modus vivendi*, is in full accordance with the institutionally informed preferences on policy design harboured by the labour market rationale.

Likewise amassing funds centrally with a view to subsequent disbursement to individuals and subordinate agencies fares well with the set of preferences embraced by the state power rationale. This is regardless of the fact that member states are likely to guard their prerogatives in this realm jealously.

## 4.2   Labour Market Integration

Western economies are facing the dual challenge of having to cope with new technologies and new patterns of production. This thrust for structural change has been one of the main forces behind European integration in the eighties. Coping with the East Asian, and to a lesser extent, the North American challenge, prompted the calls for abolishing barriers to intra-European trade. A new market dynamic was needed if European industry in strategic sectors like micro-electronics, bio-technology and new materials was to be able to constitute a relatively autonomous supply-base for European manufacturing at large. The Japanese and Korean domination in a number of components and even some application areas threatened to deny European industries, dependent on these technologies for their global competitiveness, access to the necessary supplies.

Major job generators like the automobile and aerospace industries were thus at risk. The response was an attempt to alter the dynamics of the European market place by allowing increased competition on the European level and increased flexibility at the national level.

But merely eliminating barriers to trade does not create a genuine single market with a common growth dynamic. Markets are shaped by institutions. The ability of markets to sustain stable growth patterns and their capacity to accommodate structural change is highly dependent on their institutional configuration. If Europe is to develop a genuinely single market, key institutions governing public intervention and the most crucial factor markets need to be transcended to the supranational level.

The mode of interest intermediation is a central institutional property of any modern economic system in particular when the subject matter regulated by a given pattern of intermediation is one of the key factor markets.

In the case of industrial relations there is a causal relationship between the configuration of the industrial relations system and the structure and functioning of labour markets and consequently the costs induced upon companies when pursuing structural change strategies.

Measured on variables like recruitment patterns, the possibility of reallocating labour, the flexibility of the shopfloor, the qualification process and finally dismissals and labour turnover, the structure and functioning of labour markets on the enterprise level seems to depend on:

- job control: who has it and at what level does it operate
- the structure of qualifications and jobs within the company
- organisational mode of labour

- the pattern of interest representation
- conflict regulation and the degree of formal regulation within industrial relations[215]

In listing the determinants of the structure and functioning of labour markets an ascending order starting at the shop floor and ending on the national level appears. This is not to imply a causal link. In fact the direction of the causal relation is a major subject of dispute in the literature on the political economy of interest intermediation.

In sum, major European countries on comparative levels of economic development, and highly integrated through the EU, persisted to perform differently on the global market in spite of apparent convergence in government–industry relations, finance–industry relations and last but not least, industrial relations.

This can be attributed to differences in the social foundations of macro socio-political institutions across Europe. David Soskice, among many, has drawn attention to the operation of 'institutional infrastructures' which predisposes individual societies towards specific modes of policy making.[216] Soskice points to the duration of, and level of trust in, relations between societal actors and the state as being of particular importance in shaping the general political environment.

Accordingly, the demise of high salience intermediation institutions as found in the neo-corporatist settings of North-western Europe in the mid-seventies has not resulted in competitive pluralism but rather a decentralised yet negotiated polity designated by Soskice as a 'flexibly co-ordinated system'. Extending this model to the EU at large is what key proponents of the social dimension are seeking to do.

Essentially the aspiration of current EU labour market policy is to create a 'European mode of production' with shopfloor implication by means of initiating a series of social dialogues on both European and firm level.[217]

Creating a 'European mode of production' with shopfloor implication by means of initiating tripartite roundtable discussions in Brussels is not the most viable of approaches towards enhancing Europe's overall competitive position, but as the main sponsor behind this strategy is located far from both corporate boardrooms and national government, it does seem to follow a certain twisted logic.

This logic rests on the sort of 'market constructivism' implied in the money market rationale. While the commodification of labour inherent in attempts to approach EU labour policy as market integration does reflect pure market virtues, this perspective on the social dimension mainly subscribes to the 'social embeddedness of markets'-ideal expounded by the money rationale.

### 4.3 EU's Social Dimension Towards the Year 2000: Micro-Institutional Re-Design Through Participation

Two opposing mixes of rationales each advocate their scenario on the future social dimension of the EU. Recent policy advances indicate that the latter, stressing micro-institutional re-design through participation, has prevailed.

The adoption by the Council of Directive 94/95/EC on 22 September 1994 is illustrative of the types of policies waiting ahead. The directive established the European Works Councils. In essence the directive stipulates that management and labour in European-wide undertakings shall establish forums of dialogue. Phrased in very vague terms the directive confers little in the way of authority to the settings. Once again initiating venues for mutual learning is considered sufficient.

In short this approach seeks to establish formal procedures which in turn create practices. These practices are eventually to result in the emergence of institutions in the sense of broadly recognised modes of interaction between labour and management.

This approach is as far removed from the policies of redistribution encompassed by the social democratic experience informed by the labour market rationale. Yet it is EU labour market policy nonetheless.

It is important to stress that all rationales – and the two mixes identified – can accommodate a social dimension. In conclusion, what is at stake is not the *existence* of an EU social dimension, but its *contents*.

# Notes

1 Prioritetsområdet europæisk og international udvikling 'Det mang-foldige Europa: nationale kulturer og institutioner som styrke og svaghed i den europæiske integrationsproces'. Research programme co-ordinated by Staffan Zetterholm running from June 1993 to July 1996 (J. Nr. 14-6329).

2 Kluth, Michael: 'Why a Social Dimension? An Inquiry into the Politics of European Labour Market Integration', *PhD.-afhandlinger.*, Roskilde, 1995.

3 The internal market is also denoted the Single European Market (SEM). It consists of some 300 directive proposals which can be grouped into eight different categories as follows: (1) removal of fiscal barriers, (2) free movement of labour and the right to set-up business, (3) technical harmonisation of specifications and standards, (4) liberalisation of public procurement, (5) services, (6) liberalisation of capital movements, (7) enabling cross-national industrial cooperation and (8) abolition of customs and border control. It was to come into effect by 31 December 1992.

4 The Americas host six major regional trading arrangements; besides NAFTA in the North, MERCOSUR and ANDIN in the South, Central America and the Caribbean boasts CACM, CARICOM and G3. Twenty-seven bi-, tri- or multi-lateral trade agreements have been concluded in the region since 1990. Latin America have thus long surpassed Europe and Asia with regards to growth in regional integrative ventures!

5 The issue of globalisation – and consequently regional integration – interpreted as either a process of institutional convergence or adaptation is further explored in Kluth, M. and Andersen, J.: 'Pooling the Technology Base?', 1997, Edward Elgar, in Michie, Jonathan and Howells, Jeremy (eds.): *Technology, Innovation and Competitiveness*, London, 1997a.; Kluth, M. and Andersen, J.: 'The Globalisation of European Research and Technology Organisations' forthcoming in Amin, Ash and Hausner, Jerzey (eds.): *Transforming Economies and Societies: Towards an Institutional Theory of Economic Change*, London, 1996. And finally Kluth, M. and Andersen, J.: 'Globalisation and Financial Diversity: National Approaches to the Financing of Innovative SME's' 1998, Cambridge University Press, in Archibugi, Daniele, Howells, Jeremy and Michie, Jonathan: *National Systems of Innovation or the Globalisation of Technology?*, London, 1997b.

6 Historically neofunctionalism has played a key role in relation to analysing regional integration. A thorough discussion will follow in section 2.1. Moravcsik has made a number of contributions in the field of regional integration theory. A prime example is Moravcsik, Andrew: 'Preferences and Power in the European Community: A Liberal

158

Intergovernmentalist Approach' in *Journal of Common Market Studies*, Vol. 31 No. 4, 1993.

7  Kluth, M. and Andersen, J.: *op. cit.*, 1996, 1997a and 1997b.

8  A number of theories have been developed with a view to explaining aspects of regional integration. Economic theories have mainly aimed at providing a normative justification of integration by pointing to potential benefits. See Plaschke, Henrik: *A Political Economy Approach to Regional Integration*, paper presented at CEPE, Lille, 1995. A possible exception is Balassa, Bela: 'Towards a Theory of Economic Integration', in *Kyklos*, Vol. 14, 1961. Political science contributions include: Haas, Ernst B.: *Beyond the Nation State*, Stanford, 1964a; Haas, Ernst B.: 'The Study of Regional Integration' in *International Organization*, No. 4, 1970; Wallace, William, Wallace, Helen and Webb, Carole (eds.): *Policy-Making in the European Community*, London, 1976; Pentland, Charles: *International Theory and European Integration*, New York, 1974; Lindberg, L. and Scheingold, S.: *Europe's Would-Be Polity*, New Jersey, 1970; Nye, Joseph S.: *Peace in Parts*, Boston, 1987; Harrison, Reginald J.: *Europe in Question*, London, 1974; Moravcsik, Andrew: *op. cit.*, 1993. A sociological approach was offered by Deutsch, Karl W. (et. al): *Political Community in the North Atlantic Area*, Princeton, 1957.

9  Continuity of thought in the political economy of Smith, Ricardo and Marx has been stressed by Ronald L. Meek in *Economics and Ideology and Other Essays*, London, Chapman & Hall, 1967, pp. 18–33. Taken from Bradley, Ian and Howard, Michael: 'An Introduction to Classical and Marxian Political Economy' in Bradley, I. and Howard, M. (eds.): *Classical and Marxian Political Economy*, London, Macmillan Press, 1982, p. 7. Elsewhere Meek referred to the Ricardo-Marx-Sraffa tradition which approaches value and distribution theory in a manner going beyond supply and demand analysis. Rather attention is concentrated on 'the origins, measurement and utilisation of the surplus which arises in the production activities of capitalist economic structures.' Bradley, I. and Howard, M.: *ibid.*, p. 2.

10  List, Friedrich: *The National System of Political Economy*, London (Berlin), 1909 (1841). See also Freeman, Christopher: *Technology Policy and Economic Performance – Lessons From Japan*, London, 1987.

11  Polanyi, Karl: *The Great Transformation*, Boston, 1957 (1944) p. 250.

12  Polanyi, Karl: *op. cit.* Geoffrey Hodgson makes the same point when stressing the 'necessary impurities of capitalist systems.' According to Plaschke Keynes implicitly forwarded a similar argument. Plaschke, Henrik: *op. cit.*, 1995.

13  Identifying three economic sub-systems – or markets – is by no means new. Most standard economic textbooks operate with such divisions including Branson, William H.: *Macroeconomic Theory and Policy*, New York, 1979. This distinction is also found in Samuelson, Paul A.: *Economics. An Introductory Analysis*, New York, 1969. For a very explicit analysis of the three markets as separate components in a European context, see Molle, Willem: *The Economics of European Integration – Theory, Practice, Policy*, Aldershot, 1990.

14    The term 'Imagined Communities' is taken from Anderson, B.: *Imagined Communities: Reflections on the Origins and Spread of Nationalism*, London and New York, 1983.

15    The Marxian distinction between 'Ein Klasse an sich' versus 'Ein Klasse für sich' illustrates the possible transformation of social classes from structural component to social actor.

16    The notion of 'The double Anchorage of the State' is taken from Plaschke, Henrik: *op. cit.*, 1995. It is based on Andrew Moravcsik's description of the so-called 'Two-level Games'. Moravcsik, Andrew: *op. cit.*, 1993.

17    Dyson, Kenneth: *The State Tradition in Western Europe*, Oxford, 1980. p. 51.

18    Schmitter, Philippe: 'Corporatisme and the State' in Grant, Wyn and Sargent, Jane (eds.): *The Political Economy of Neo-corporatism*, London, 1985.

19    Deutsch, Karl W. (et. al): *op. cit.*, 1957. p. 2.

20    Tönnies, Ferdinand: *Fundamental Concepts of Sociology: Gemeinschaft and Geselschaft*, New York, 1940.

21    Gellner, Ernest: *Nations and Nationalism*, Oxford, 1983.

22    Taken from Hodgson, Geoffrey M.: *Institutional Economics: A Manifesto for a Modern Institutional Economics*, Cambridge, 1988.

23    Soskice, David: 'The Institutional Infrastructures for International Competitiveness: A Comparative Analysis of the UK and Germany', Unpublished paper, Berlin, 1991.

24    See Marin, Bernd and Mayntz, Renate: *Policy Networks: Empirical Evidence and Theoretical Considerations*, Frankfurt a. M., 1991.

25    Goldstein, Judith and Keohane, Robert O.: 'Ideas and Foreign Policy: An Analytical Framework' in Goldstein, Judith and Keohane, Robert O. (eds.): *Ideas and Foreign Policy*, Cornell University Press, Ithaca, 1993.

26    Maslow, Abraham H.: *Motivation and Personality*, New York, 1954.

27    Seminal contributions by proponents of the English School include Bull, Hedley: *The Anarchical Society – A Study of Order in World Politics*, London, 1977. Bull, Hedley, Kingsbury, Benedict and Roberts, Adam (eds.): *Hugo Grotius and International Relations*, Oxford 1992 (1990). Vincent, John R.: *Human Rights and International Relations*, Cambridge, 1986.

28    For an interesting discussion see Buzan, Barry: 'From International System to International Society: Structural Realism and Regime Theory meets the English School' in *International Organization*, Vol. 47, No. 3. 1993; Neumann, Iver B. (ed.): *The 'English School' of International Relations: A Conference Report*, Oslo, 1994.

29    See for example Keohane, Robert O.: *After Hegemony – Cooperation and Discord in the World Political Economy*, Princeton, 1985.

30    Keohane, Robert O.: *op. cit.*, 1985.

31    Plaschke, Henrik: *op. cit.*, 1995.

32    Examples of the respective positions are found in Poulantzas, Nico: *State, Power, Socialism*, London, 1978. Miliband, Ralph: *Class Power and State Power*, London, 1983.

33 Laclau, Ernesto and Mouffe, Chantal: *Hegemony and Socialist Strategy*, London, 1985.
34 March, James and Olsen, Johan: *Rediscovering Institutions*, New York, 1989.
35 For an illuminating discussion (in Danish) see Dyrberg, Torben and Torfin, Jakob: 'Politik og institutioner' in *Statsvetenskaplig Tidskrift*, Vol. 2, 1992.
36 Plasckhe pursues a similar point on the basis of Hager and Hicks. According to Hager an apparently functional logic dictates that either labour or finance has to be exposed to global pressures in order to shelter the other. Plaschke, Henrik: *op. cit.*, 1995. pp. 17–21.
37 Hampdon-Turner, Michael and Vermenslar, Alfons: *The Seven Cultures of Capitalism*, London, 1992.
38 Goldstein, Judith and Keohane, Robert O. (eds.): *op. cit.*, 1993.
39 A former CEO at 'Bank of America' thus notes that 'the global financial market is a figment of the Reuters screen' (John Zysman).
40 Kluth, M. and Andersen, J.: *op. cit.*, 1997b.
41 For informative discussions on the transfer from fordism to post-fordism see the works of Aglietta, M.: *A Theory of Capitalist Regulation: The US Experience* (translated by David Fernbach), London, New Left Books, 1979. Boyer, Robert and Durand, Jean-Pierre: *After Fordism*, (translated by Sybil Hyacinth Mair), Basingstoke: Macmillan, 1997. Boyer, Robert: *The Regulation School: a Critical Introduction* (translated by Craig Cherney), New York: Columbia University Press, 1990. Jessop, Bob: 'Fordism and post-Fordism: a Critical Reformulation' in *COS forskningsrapport*, No. 16, 1990. Copenhagen: Center for Public Organization and Management, Copenhagen Business School. Jessop, Bob (et. al): *The Politics of Flexibility: Restructuring State and Industry in Britain, Germany and Scandinavia*, Aldershot: Edward Elgar, 1991. Changes in the direction of craft-centred production methods has in particular been advocated by Sable, C. and Piore, M.: *The Second Industrial Divide*, London, 1984.
42 Borrus, Michael: *The Architecture of the Supply-base*, BRIE Working Paper, Berkeley, 1993. A similar perspective is advanced in Lundvall, Bengt-Åke: 'Innovation as an Interactive Process: User-Producer Relations.' in Dosi, Giovanni et. al (eds.): *Technical Change and Economic Theory*, London, 1988.
43 For a discussion on the characteristics of social norms and their impact on economic thinking see Elster, Jon: 'Social Norms and Economic Theory' in *Journal of Economic Perspectives*, Vol. 3, No. 4, 1989.
44 Pedersen, Ove K.: *Learning Processes and the Game of Negotiation*, COS Research Report 12/1990, Copenhagen, 1990.
45 The theme of 'concerted action' is explored in the literature on neo-corporatism. See in particular Lehmbruch, Gerhard: 'Liberal Corporatism and Party Government' in *Comparative Political Studies*, No. 10, 1977; Grant, Wyn (ed.): *The Political Economy of Corporatism*, London, 1985; Williamson, Peter J.: *Varieties of Corporatism*, Cambridge, 1985; Cawson, A.: *Corporatism and Political Theory*, Oxford, 1986; Windmuller, John P. (et. al): *Collective Bargaining in*

*Industrialized Economies: A Reappraisal*, Geneva, 1987; Williamson, Peter J.: *Corporatism in Perspective*, London, 1989; Streeck, Wolfgang and Schmitter, Philip C.: 'From National Corporatism to Transnational Pluralism' in *Politics and Society*, No. 2, 1991.

46  Kluth, Michael: *op. cit.*, 1995.

47  Hotz-Hart, Beat: 'Comparative Research and New Technology: Modernisation in Three Industrial Relations Systems' in Hyman, R. and Streeck, W. (eds.): *New Technology and Industrial Relations*, Oxford, 1988, p. 63.

48  This applies to, e.g., Karel Engliš and John Hicks.

49  Zysman, John: *Governments, Markets and Growth*, Oxford, 1983, p. 5.

50  Kluth, M. and Andersen, J.: *op. cit.*, 1997b.

51  There is ample evidence in support of this observation. Reference is usually made to the by now classical 'Luton Study' where the 'affluent workers' in British manufacturing industry where shown to undergo changes in social values.

52  This point receives comprehensive attention in some of Joseph A. Schumpeter's last works including Schumpeter, Joseph A.: *Capitalism, Socialism and Democracy*, New York, 1946. See also Swedeberg, R.: *Joseph A. Schumpeter – His Life and Work*, Cambridge, 1991.

53  The latter was characteristic of the social dimension of the European Coal and Steel Community.

54  This is the core statement of the 'National Systems of Innovation' literature.

55  These insights have in particular been propagated by the so-called 'French Regulation School'. For similar statements generated within American academic traditions, see works coming out of Berkeley's Roundtable on the International Economy (BRIE).

56  The question of the designability of institutions is disputed. James March and Johan Olsen are hesitant, others – such as Ernesto Laclau and Chantal Mouffe – implicitly designate more latitude for intentional design.

57  In direct opposition to the above, Aron Wildavsky has formulated a 'counter-Wagner' law which stipulates that high growth economies need not raise the level of taxation in order to provide the revenues needed to meet public demand for services. The rising income levels will thus in themselves provide the necessary means required to fund public services. Countries with modest growth levels, like the United Kingdom, will accordingly need to raise tax levels in order to finance increased public demand.

58  Dunleavy, Patrick and O'Leary, Brendan: *Theories of the State*, Macmillan, London, 1987, p. 64.

59  Levy, Jonah: 'After Etatisme: Dilemmas of institutional reform in post-dirigiste France', final chapter in *Toqueville's Revenge: Dilemmas of Institution Building in Post-dirigiste France*, PhD Dissertation, Political Science Department, University of California, Berkeley, 1994. See also Dunleavy, P. and O'Leary, B.: *op. cit.*, 1987, p. 65.

60  Subramaniam, V.: 'Representative Bureaucracy: A Reassessment' in *American Political Science Review*, Vol. 61, No. 4, 1967, pp. 1010–19.

Taken from Dunleavy, P. and O'Leary, B.: *op. cit.*, 1987.

61 Birnbaum, P.: *The Heights of Power*, Chicago, 1981.

62 Kluth, M. and Andersen, J: *op. cit.*, 1994.

63 Freeman, Chris: *The Economics of Technical Change*, London, 1974.

64 Haas, Ernst B.: 'Technocracy, Pluralism and the New Europe' in Graubard, Stephen R. (ed.): *A New Europe?*, Boston, 1964b, pp. 64–6.

65 Keohane, Robert O. and Hoffman, Stanley: *op. cit.*, 1990.

66 For an excellent overview of the structure of the Commission and other institutions see Nugent, Neill: *The Government and Politics of the European Community*, London, 1990. In addition Coombes's study of the CEU remains a reference point for research on Commission affairs. Coombes, David: *Politics and Bureaucracy in the European Community*, London, 1970.

67 Feld, Werner: 'National Economic Interest Groups and Policy Formation in the EEC' in *Political Science Quarterly*, No. 2, 1966, p. 402.

68 Commission des Communautés européennes: *Répertoire des organisations professionnelles de la CEE*, Brussels, 1986, p. 8. According to Werner Feld, the CEU informally consults extensively with certain key national interest organisations. Feld, Werner: *op. cit.*, 1966. And Averyt, William: 'Eurogroups, Clientela and the European Community' in *International Organization*, No. 4, 1975.

69 Meeting the 'coherence requirement' has not been easy for the Parliament. In relation to, for example, bio-technology legislation, the plenary session underscored the negotiated settlement between its own conciliation committee and the Council as in March 1995 it voted down a proposal (240–188) which had been 7 years and numerous compromises under way.

70 On 27 April 1990, seven so-called independent unions from EU and EFTA countries alike, founded the Confederation Européenne des Syndicats Independents (CESI). The total of approximately four million members are mainly academically trained civil servants or professionals. Data on CESI can be found in Andersen, Svein S. and Eliassen, Kjell A.: *Trade Union Influence in the European Community*, Sandvika, 1991.

71 A number of European business organisations also handle the role of employer peak organisation. These organisations typically represent major segments of the service industries and have no affiliation to UNICE which mainly represents manufacturing industry. Some of the biggest business organisations outside the UNICE framework co-ordinate general boundary crossing issues at the EU level with the UNICE in the Employers Liaison Committee (ELC).

72 For a thorough account of ETUC history see Barnouin, Barbara: *The European Labour Movement and European Integration*, London, 1986.

73 ETUI: 'The European Trade Union Confederation: ETUC' in *ETUI Info*, No. 29, 1990.

74 See chapter 3.

75 Yet national experiences on interest group–state relations diverge. For a survey of business interests and their interaction with government

under conditions ranging from clientelism to neo-corporatism see
Lehmbruch, Gerhard and Schmitter, Philip (eds.): *Patterns of
Corporatist Policy-Making*, London, 1982.

76   Streeck, W. and Schmitter, Philip C.: *op. cit.*, 1991.
77   The founding Treaties of the Union contained specific reference to
labour market issues. Besides unbinding references in the Preamble,
the Treaty of Rome contained a title on social policy (part III, title III).
This title comprises articles 117–122 and a chapter on the European
Social Fund. Article 118 is by far the most widely quoted treaty provision when the Union's action in the field is to be given legal substance,
it stipulates fields where the Commission of the European Union
(CEU) shall attempt to stimulate cooperation between states. No legal
bases towards the accomplishment of these aims are, however, offered.
Article 119 is the most precise of the general labour and social policy
provisions. It deals with equal treatment of men and women. Articles
relating to measures for the retraining and relocation of labour subject
to sectorial adjustments can be found in the Paris and the Rome
Treaties. These provisions were, however, tightly linked to the adjust-
ment requirements of the coal and steel industries and, to a lesser
extent, agriculture. No clear distinction is made between social policy
and labour market policy in the original Treaty. Article 51 under
chapter 1, title III, part 2 thus transcends into the sphere of social
policy in that it stipulates the basic principle of guaranteeing certain
mobile labour rights with regard to transferability of earned social enti-
tlements and the possibility of receiving social security in other
member states.
78   ILO: 'Social Aspects of European Collaboration', *ILO Studies and
Reports*, No. 46 (new series), Geneva, 1956.
79   See, for example, Nielsen, Ruth and Szyszczak, Erika: *The Social
Dimension of the European Community*, Copenhagen, 1991.
80   Blanpain, Roger: *Labour Law and Industrial Relations of the European
Community*, Deventer, 1991, p. 143.
81   Obst, Wolfgang: 'The Safety and Health Commission for the Mining
and Other Extractive Industries: a Double Role' in *Social Europe*,
No. 2, 1990, p. 64.
82   Blanpain, Roger: *op. cit.*, 1991, p. 143.
83   A truly common product market encompassing capital goods is only
now emerging with the comming into effect of the internal market
scheme. National champions, it appears, have all but lost their political
patrons in Paris, Bonn, Rome and London.
84   Nielsen, Ruth and Szyszczak, Erika: *The Social Dimension of the
European Community*, Copenhagen, 1991, p. 27.
85   Morettini: Yves: 'Advisory Committee on Safety, Hygiene and Health
Protection at Work' in *Social Europe*, No. 2, 1990, p. 14.
86   Hunter, W. J.: 'Preface' in *Social Europe*, No. 2, 1990, p. 7.
87   Nielsen, Ruth and Szyszczak, Erika: *op. cit.*, 1991, pp. 184–85.
88   Streeck, Wolfgang and Schmitter, Philip C.: 'From National
Corporatism to Transnational Pluralism' in *Politics and Society*, 1991,
No. 2.

89 Streeck, Wolfgang and Schmitter, Philip C.: *ibid.*, 1991, No. 2.
90 Teague, Paul and Grahl, John: 'The European Community Social Charter and Labour Market Regulation.' in *Journal of Public Policies*, No. 2, 1992, p. 226.
91 National standardisation bodies have formed joint committees at the European level. Some sectors, like aerospace and telecommunication, have established sectorial committees, but most branches of manufacturing industry are encompassed by the two main European bodies CENELEC (Comité Européen de la Normalisation du Electro-Technic), covering electro- and electromechanical industry, and CEN (Comité Européen de la Normalisation) covering all other types of industry.
92 Interview, Copenhagen, March 1991.
93 Interview, Copenhagen, November 1991.
94 CEU: *Europas Sociale Dimension*, Luxembourg, 1989, p. 37.
95 CEU: *Forslag til Rådets Direktiv om ændring af direktiv 89/392/EØF*, Brussels, December 1989b, p. 3.
96 CEU: *op. cit.*, December 1989b, p. 5.
97 CEU: *op. cit.*, December 1989b, p. 6.
98 Interview, Brussels, June 1992.
99 Interview, Copenhagen, November 1991.
100 Kluth, Michael: *op. cit.*, 1995.
101 As of 23 December 1993 42 measures had been proposed by the CEU under the SAP. Of these, 25 were directives. Of the 25 directives, 14 relate to health and safety excluding 348/92/EEC on the protection of pregnant women at the workplace which the CEU insists falls under the heading 'Equal treatment for men and women.' Source: DA (Danish Employer Association): 'Bilag' in *DA-International*, 23 December 1993b.
102 Nielsen, Ruth and Szyszczak, Erika: *op. cit.*, 1991, p. 162.
103 Blanpain, Roger: *op. cit.*, 1991, pp. 146–51.
104 Blanpain, Roger: *op. cit.*, 1991, p. 150.
105 Environmental Resources Limited: 'The Impact of the Occupational Health and Safety Legislation of the European Community on Development of Legislation in the Member States' in *Social Europe*, No. 2, 1990, p. 9.
106 See Thematic Issue of *The International Journal of Comparative Labour Law and Industrial Relations*, No. 6, 1990.
107 Biagi, M.: 'From Conflict to Participation in Safety: Industrial Relations and the Working Environment in Europe 1992' and Weiss, M.: 'The Industrial Relations of Occupational Health: The Impact of the Framework Directive on the Federal Republic of Germany' both appearing in *The International Journal of Comparative Labour Law and Industrial Relations*, No. 6, 1990.
108 Council Directive 89/391/EEC, Article 11, first indent.
109 Council Directive 89/391/EEC, Article 11.
110 Morettini: Yves: *op. cit.*, 1990, pp. 20–22.
111 Interview, Brussels, June 1992.
112 See articles by Brun, François – Ministry of Labour, France; Konstanty,

Rheinhold – DGB Federal Executive, Social Policy Division, German Trade Union Federation; Eberlie, R. F. – Director, British Confederation of Industry, Brussels Office. All in *Social Europe*, 1990, No. 2, pp. 23–25.

113   Morettini: Yves: *op. cit.*, 1990, p. 17.
114   Morettini: Yves: *op. cit.*, 1990, p. 20.
115   Interview, Brussels, July 1992.
116   Eberlie, R. F.: *op. cit.*, 1990, p. 25.
117   Interview, London, September 1992.
118   Interview, Copenhagen, November 1991.
119   Teague, Paul and Grahl, John: *op. cit.*, 1992, p. 227.
120   Interview, Brussels, September 1992.
121   Carrol, John F.: 'The Constructive Role of the Economic and Social Committee as Regards Safety and Health at the Workplace' in *Social Europe*, No. 2, 1990, p. 29.
122   Meehan, Elizabeth: *Citizenship and the European Community*, London, 1993, p. 68.
123   Commission Decision of 9 December 1981 found in *Social Europe*, No. 3, 1991, pp. 158–60.
124   'Europæiske arbejdsgivere og lønmodtagere vil ændre EF-udvalg' in *DA International*, 18 February 1993.
125   Directives: 75/117/EEC – Equal Pay, 76/207/EEC – Equal Treatment in Employment etc., 79/7/EEC – Equality in Social Security, 86/378/EEC – Equality in Occupational Social Security Schemes, 86/613/EEC – Equality for Self-employed including Protection of Self-employed Women during Pregnancy.
126   Docksey, C.: 'The European Community and the Promotion of Equality' in McCrudden, C. (ed.): *Women, Employment and European Equality Law*, London, 1987, p. 1.
127   CEU: *Social Europe*, No. 3, 1991, p. 15
128   A number of cross-national panels were established containing social policy evaluators. The activities of these panels were sponsored by the Commission.
129   Nielsen, Ruth and Szyszczak, Erika: *op. cit.*, 1991, pp. 129–30.
130   Venturini, Patrick: 1992: *Det Sociale Perspektiv.*, Luxembourg, 1989.
131   Teague, Paul and Grahl, John: *op. cit.*, 1992, p. 212.
132   See also Teague, Paul and Grahl, John: *op. cit.*, 1992, p. 212.
133   François Staedelin: 'Social Policy, Social Charter, Basic Rights' in *Social Europe*, No. 1, 1990, p. 21.
134   Teague, Paul and Grahl, John: *op. cit.*, 1992, p. 212.
135   Interviews, Brussels, June, September 1992 and London, September 1992.
136   Interview, Brussels, September 1992.
137   The completion date for the action programme was thus changed from June 1990 to December 1989. Interview, Brussels, April 1992.
138   The proposed directives concerned: work time, pregnant women, information and hearing of labour in multinational corporations, labour contracts plus three proposals regarding the regulation of atypical work contracts.

139 Nielsen, Ruth and Szyszczak, Erika: *op. cit.*, 1991, p. 131.
140 Interview, Brussels, September 1992.
141 Interview, Brussels, September 1992.
142 This phrasing was repeatedly used by UNICE officials. Interviews, Brussels, April and May 1992.
143 Pedersen, Ove K.: *op. cit.*, 1990.
144 Pluralist democratic theory is first and foremost identified with Robert A. Dahl. Classics in the genre include Dahl, R. A.: *Who Governs?: Democracy and Power in an American City*, New Haven, 1961; Dahl, R. A. and Lindblom, Charles: *Politics, Economics and Welfare*, New York, 1953 and 1976 (2nd edn).
145 While this alignment was unfair and ideologically dubious, it did create what Peter Williamson has denoted a 'guilt by association'. Peter, Williamson: *Varieties of Corporatism*, Cambridge, 1985.
146 Interview, Brussels, 1992.
147 The decline in overall French Union power accelerated throughout the eighties. In the fifties, when the ESC was set up, the country enjoyed a unionisation rate comparable to Germany. See Lane, J. E., McKay, D. and Newton, K.: *Political Data Handbook: OECD Countries*, Oxford, 1991, pp. 25–26.
148 Bagolioni, Guido and Crouch, Colin (eds.): *European Industrial Relations*, London, 1990.
149 Gullman, Claus and Hagel-Sørensen, Karsten.: *EF-ret*, Copenhagen, 1989.
150 'The European Social Dialogue within Sectors' in *Social Europe*, No. 5, 1985, pp. 9–14.
151 Kirchner, Emil: *Trade Unions as a Pressure Group in The European Community*, Westmead, Hants, 1977, p. 107.
152 Mclaughlin, D.: 'The Involvement of the Social Partners at the European Level' in Vandamme, J.: *New Dimensions in European Social Policy*, London, 1985, p. 157.
153 A directory was published in 1986. It is, however, incomplete and contains no information regarding the composition of the committees. The Commission of the European Communities: *Comites*, Brussels, 1986.
154 Interview, Brussels, June 1992.
155 'The European Social Dialogue within Sectors' in *Social Europe*, No. 5, 1985, p. 11.
156 'The European Social Dialogue within Sectors' in *op. cit.*, 1985, p. 12.
157 See, for example, Keegan, William: *Mr. Lawson's Gamble*, London, 1989, Molle, William: *The Economics of European Integration*, Aldershot, 1990. Allum, Percy: *State and Society in Western Europe*, Cambridge, 1995.
158 And indeed technical spillover pressures never really materialised. I have argued elsewhere that this can be attributed to the limited quantities of labourers moving about and the political weakness of mobile labourers. Usually originating in regions with poor trade union activity, in addition to confinement to the bottom echelons of the labour market due to lacking skills, European migrant workers as a group appeared little capable of pushing their demands on the Brussels agenda. See Kluth, Michael: *op. cit.*, 1995.

159   The semi-ideological role of neo-functionalism in the Brussels arena has been observed by several scholars. A case in point is Sweeney, Jane P.: *The First European Elections*, Washington, 1980.

160   Urwin, Derek, W.: The Community of Europe, Harlow, 1991, pp. 135–39.

161   The neo-corporatist literature is extremely diverse. Philippe Schmitter is accredited with setting off the neo-corporatist charge on pluralism with his article 'Still the Century of Corporatism' in *Review of Politics*, Vol. 36, 1974.

162   Following the advance of the 'dual polity thesis' a more modest understanding gained recognition. In the 'meso-corporatist' formula corporatist settings at sectorial and regional levels co-exist with a national pluralist system entrusted with the task of binding sectorial policies to a tentatively coherent whole. Alan Cawson has made a major contribution to this perspective in his book: *Corporatism and Political Theory*, Oxford, 1986.

163   Heisler, Martin O.: 'Corporate Pluralism Revisited: Where is the Theory?' in *Scandinavian Political Studies*, No. 3, 1979, p. 282.

164   Williamson, Peter J.: *op. cit.*, 1985, p. 137.

165   Crouch, Colin: 'Pluralism and the New Corporatism: A Rejoinder' in *Political Studies*, Vol. XXXI, 1983, pp. 452–60.

166   Streeck, Wolfgang and Schmitter, Philippe C.: *op. cit.*, 1991.

167   Following the adoption of Regulation 1612/68 and Directive 360/68.

168   This proposition is convincingly advanced by Streeck, Wolfgang and Schmitter, Philippe C.: *op. cit.*, 1991.

169   Precursors of this school may be found in Andrew Shonfield's analysis of economic management in Germany. See Shonfield, Andrew: *Modern Capitalism*, Oxford, 1965.

170   Prominent advocates of this approach include: Gudmund Hernes, Norway and Ove Kaj Pedersen and Klaus Nielsen, Denmark.

171   Bernd, Marin and Mayntz, Renate: *op. cit.*, 1991.

172   Lundvall, Bengt-Åke: *The Learning Economy – Challenges to Economic Theory and Policy*, unpublished paper presented at the EAEPE Conference, Copenhagen 1994.

173   Venturini, Patrick: *op. cit.*, 1989, p. 66.

174   Monggaard, Dorte: 'Ny europæisk overenskomst' in *LO-Bladet*, No. 25, 1990.

175   Savoini, Carlo: 'The Social Dialogue in the Community' in *Social Europe* No. 2, 1984, p. 9.

176   Barnouin, Barbara: *op. cit.*, 1986, p. 118.

177   Savoini, Carlo: *op. cit.*, 1984, p. 9.

178   Savoini, Carlo: *op. cit.*, 1984, p. 9.

179   Savoini, Carlo: *op. cit.*, 1984, p. 9.

180   Savoini, Carlo: *op. cit.*, 1984, pp. 9–12.

181   CEU, DG V: 'Joint Opinions', *European Social Dialogue Documentary Series*, Luxembourg, 1991, pp. 18–21.

182   Carley, Mark: 'Social Dialogue' in Gold, M (ed.): *The Social Dimension*, London, 1993, p. 117.

183   CEU, DG V: *op. cit.*, 1991, p. 37.

184   CEU, DG V: *op. cit.*, 1991, pp. 19–20.

185 Interviews in Brussels, June 1992.

186 Carley, Mark: *op. cit.*, 1993, p. 115.

187 Tromborg, Per: *Den Sociale Dimension*, unpublished paper, University of Roskilde, 1991.

188 Interview, Copenhagen, January 1991.

189 Carley, Mark: *op. cit.*, 1993, p. 115.

190 Carley, Mark: *op. cit.*, 1993, p. 116.

191 CEU, DG V: *op. cit.*, 1991, p. 82.

192 Whether the setting will be able to produce a substantial policy is a different matter.

193 Interviews, London, September 1992.

194 Both the official periodical 'Social Europe' and the above-mentioned publications issued by the CEU on the social dialogue contain ample evidence hereof.

195 Jessop, Bob: *From the Keynesian Welfare State to the Schumpeterian Workfare State*, unpublished paper, 1992.

196 Interview in Brussels, July 1992.

197 Interview in Brussels, September 1992.

198 CEU DG V: *op. cit.*, 1991, p. 20.

199 Savoini, Carlo: *op. cit.*, 1984, p. 11.

200 Savoini, Carlo: *op. cit.*, 1984, p. 11.

201 Barnouin, Barbara: *op. cit.*, 1986, pp. 90–95.

202 The CEU's role as initiator for the establishment of dialogue institutions can only be determined for those bodies not covered by the original Treaties.

203 Interview, Brussels and London, September 1992 and Copenhagen, January 1991.

204 Holloway, J.: *Social Policy Harmonisation in the European Community*, Aldershot, 1981.

205 In Ross, George: *Jacques Delors and European Integration*, Cambridge, 1995, the term 'Delorism' is introduced referring to an understanding of society, governance and EU development in line with the argument outlined above.

206 See for example Lange, Peter: 'The Politics of the Social Dimension' in Sbragia, Alberta: *The Political Consequences of 1992 for the European Community*, Washington DC, 1992.

207 Soskice, David: *op. cit.*, 1991.

208 Streeck, Wolfgang: *Social Institutions and Economic Performance: Studies of Industrial Relations in Advanced Capitalist Economies*, London, 1992.

209 Marin, Bernd and Mayntz, Renate: *op. cit.*, 1991.

210 Lange, Peter: *op. cit.*, 1992, pp. 254–55

211 E.g. Sable, C. and Piore, M.: *op. cit.*, 1984.

212 The concerted action of the seventies did – in its most successful implementations – produce some wage restraint, a lowering of national health and safety standards on grounds of competitiveness has of yet not been observed in any OECD country. Although the quest for labour market flexibility caused some decay in established labour market rules and procedures, these related to forms of employment

rather than the physical conditions of the work place. Even though short-term and part-time contracts were increasingly put to use there is little, if any, evidence of a deterioration of health and safety standards in the member states of the European Union in this period attributable to internal or external competitive pressure.

213 Porter, Michael: *The Competitive Advantage of Nations*, New York, 1990.

214 Yet allowing foreign contractors cross-border access to neighbouring markets will inevitably lead to clashes with labour in regions being net recipients of such services. Consequently separate regulation has been enacted to handle the delicate problems of cross-border labour issues.

215 Hotz-Hart, Beat: 'Comparative Research and New Technology: Mordernization in Three Industrial Relations Systems' in Hyman, R. and Streek, W. (eds.): *New Technology and Industrial Relations*, Oxford, 1988, p. 63.

216 Soskice, David: *op. cit.*, 1991.

217 See for example Lange, Peter: *op. cit.*, 1992.

# References

Allum, Percy: *State and Society in Western Europe*, Cambridge, 1995.

Andersen, Svein S. and Eliassen, Kjell A.: *The Explosion of European Community Lobbying*, Sandvika (Report 1990-316-7), 1990.

Andersen, Svein S. and Eliassen, Kjell A.: *Trade Union Influence in the European Community*, Sandvika (Working Paper), 1991.

Anderson, B.: *Imagined Communities: Reflections on the Origins and Spread of Nationalism*, London and New York, 1983.

Averyt, William: 'Eurogroups, Clientela and the European Community', *International Organization*, No. 4, 1975.

Bagolioni, Guido and Crouch, Colin (eds.): *European Industrial Relations*, London, 1990.

Balassa, Bela: 'Towards a Theory of Economic Integration', in *Kyklos*, Vol. 14, 1961.

Barnouin, Barbara: *The European Labour Movement and European Integration*, London, 1986.

Biagi, M.: 'From Conflict to Participation in Safety: Industrial Relations and the Working Environment in Europe 1992' in *The International Journal of Comparative Labour Law and Industrial Relations*, No. 6, 1990.

Birnbaum, P.: *The Heights of Power*, Chicago, 1981.

Blanpain, Roger: *Labour Law and Industrial Relations of the European Community*, Deventer, 1991.

Borrus, Michael: *The Architecture of the Supply-base*, BRIE Working Paper, Berkeley, 1993.

Bradley, Ian and Howard, Michael: 'An Introduction to Classical and Marxian Political Economy' in Bradley, I. and Howard, M. (eds.): *Classical and Marxian Political Economy*, London, Macmillan, 1982.

Branson, William H.: *Macroeconomic Theory and Policy*, New York, 1979.

Bull, Hedley: *The Anarchical Society – A Study of Order in World Politics*, London, 1977.

Bull, Hedley, Kingsbury, Benedict and Roberts, Adam (eds.): *Hugo Grotius and International Relations*, Oxford 1992 [1990].

Buzan, Barry: 'From International System to International Society: Structural Realism and Regime Theory meets the English School' in *International Organization*, Vol. 47, No. 3, 1993.

Carley, Mark: 'Social Dialogue' in Gold, M (ed.): *The Social Dimension*, London, 1993.

Carrol, John F.: 'The Constructive Role of the Economic and Social Committee as Regards Safety and Health at the Workplace' in *Social Europe*, No. 2, 1990.

Cawson, A.: *Corporatism and Political Theory*, Oxford, 1986.

CEU: *Europas Sociale Dimension*, Luxembourg, 1989.

CEU: *Forslag til Rådets Direktiv om ændring af direktiv 89/392/EØF*, Brussels, December 1989b.

Commission des Communautés européennes: *Répertoire des organisations professionnelles de la CEE*, Brussels, 1986.

Commission des Communautés européennes: *Comites*, Brussels, 1986.

CEU (DGV): 'Joint Opinions', *European Social Dialogue Documentary Series*, Luxembourg, 1991.

Coombes, David: *Politics and Bureaucracy in the European Community*, London, 1970.

Crouch, Colin: 'Pluralism and the New Corporatism: A Rejoinder', *Political Studies*, Vol. XXXI, 1983.

DA (Danish Employer Association): 'Europæiske arbejdsgivere og lønmodtagere vil ændre EF-udvalg' in *DA International*, 18 February 1993.

DA (Danish Employer Association): 'Bilag' in *DA-International*, 23 December 1993.

Dahl, R. A.: *Who Governs?: Democracy and Power in an American City*, New Haven, 1961.

Dahl, R. A. and Lindblom, Charles: *Politics, Economics and Welfare*, New York, 1953 and 1976 (2nd edn).

Deutsch, Karl W. (et. al): *Political Community in the North Atlantic Area*, Princeton, 1957.

Docksey, C.: 'The European Community and the Promotion of Equality' in McCrudden, C. (ed.): *Women, Employment and European Equality Law*, London, 1987.

Dunleavy, Patrick and O'Leary, Brendan: *Theories of the State*, Macmillan, London, 1987.

Dyrberg, Torben and Torfin, Jakob: 'Politik og institutioner' in *Statsvetenskaplig Tidskrift*, Vol. 2, 1992.

Dyson, Kenneth: *The State Tradition in Western Europe*, Oxford, 1980.

Elster, Jon: 'Social Norms and Economic Theory' in *Journal of Economic Perspectives*, Vol. 3, No. 4, 1989.

Environmental Resources Limited: 'The Impact of the Occupational Health and Safety Legislation of the European Community on Development of Legislation in the Member States', in *Social Europe*, No. 2, 1990.

Esping-Andersen, Gøsta: *Politics against Markets: The Social Democratic Road to Power*, Princeton, 1985.

Esping-Andersen, Gösta: *The Three Worlds of Welfare Capitalism*, Cornwall, 1990.

ETUI: 'The European Trade Union Confederation: ETUC' in *ETUI Info*, No. 29, 1990.

Feld, Werner: 'National Economic Interest Groups and Policy Formation in the EEC', *Political Science Quarterly*, No. 2, 1966.

Freeman, Christopher: *The Economics of Technical Change*, London, 1974.

Freeman, Christopher: *Technology Policy and Economic Performance: Lessons from Japan*, London, 1987.

Gellner, Ernest: *Nations and Nationalism*, Oxford, 1983.

Goldstein, Judith and Keohane, Robert O.: 'Ideas and Foreign Policy: An Analytical Framework' in Goldstein, Judith and Keohane, Robert O. (eds.): *Ideas and Foreign Policy*, Cornell University Press, Ithaca, 1993.

Grant, Wyn (ed.): *The Political Economy of Corporatism*, London, 1985.

Gullman, Claus and Hagel-Sørensen, Karsten: *EF-ret*, Copenhagen, 1989.

Haas, Ernst B.: *Beyond the Nation State*, Stanford, 1964a.

Haas, Ernst B: 'Technocracy, Pluralism and the New Europe', in Stephen R. Graubard (ed.): *A New Europe?*, Boston, 1964b.

Haas, Ernst B.: 'The Study of Regional Integration', *International Organization*, No. 4, 1970.

Hague, Rod and Harrop, Martin: *Comparative Government – An Introduction*, London, 1985.

Hampdon-Turner, Michael and Vermenslar, Alfons: *The Seven Cultures of Capitalism*, London, 1992.

Harrison, Reginald J.: *Europe in Question*, London, 1974.

Heclo, Hugo: *A Government of Strangers: Executive Politics in Washington*, Brookings Institute, 1977.

Heisler, Martin O.: 'Corporate Pluralism Revisited: Where is the Theory?', *Scandinavian Political Studies*, No. 3, 1979.

Hodgson, Geoffrey M.: *Institutional Economics: A Manifesto for a Modern Institutional Economics*, Cambridge, 1988.

Holloway, J.: *Social Policy Harmonisation in the European Community*, Aldershot, 1981.

Hotz-Hart, Beat: 'Comparative Research and New Technology: Modernisation in Three Industrial Relations Systems' in Hyman, R. and Streeck, W. (eds.): *New Technology and Industrial Relations*, Oxford 1988.

Hunter, W. J.: 'Preface', in *Social Europe*, 1990.

ILO: 'Social Aspects of European Collaboration', *ILO Studies and Reports*, No. 46 (new series), Geneva, 1956.

Jessop, Bob: *From the Keynesian Welfare State to the Schumpeterian Workfare State*, unpublished paper, 1992.

Keegan, William: *Mr. Lawson's Gamble*, London, 1989.

Keohane, Robert O.: *After Hegemony – Cooperation and Discord in the World Political Economy*, Princeton, 1985.

Kirchner, Emil: *Trade Unions as a Pressure Group in the European Community*, Westmead, Hants, 1977.

Kluth, Michael F.: 'Why a Social Dimension? – An Inquiry into the Politics of European Labour Market Integration', *PhD.-afhandlinger*, Roskilde, 1995.

Kluth, Michael F. and Andersen, Jørn B.: 'The Globalisation of European Research and Technology Organisations', forthcoming in Ash, A. and Hausner, J. (eds.): *Transforming Economies and Societies: Towards an Institutional Theory of Economic Change*, Edward Elgar, London, 1997.

Kluth, Michael F. and Andersen, Jørn B.: 'Pooling the Technology Base?', forthcoming in Michie, J. and Howells, J. (eds.): *Technology, Innovation and Competitiveness*, Edward Elgar, London, 1997a.

Kluth, Michael F. and Andersen, Jørn B.: 'Globalisation and Financial Diversity: The Making of Venture Capital Markets in France, Germany and UK' forthcoming in Archibugi, Daniele, Howells, Jeremy and Michie, Jonathan (eds.): *National Systems of Innovation or the Globalisation of Technology?*, London, 1997b.

Korpi, Walter: *The Working Class in Welfare Capitalism: Work, Unions and Politics in Sweden*, London, Routledge & Kegan Paul, 1978.

Laclau, Ernesto and Mouffe, Chantal: *Hegemony and Socialist Strategy*, London, 1985.

Lane, J.E., McKay, D. and Newton, K.: *Political Data Handbook: OECD Countries*, Oxford, 1991.

Lange, Peter: 'The Politics of the Social Dimension' in Sbragia, Alberta M.: *The Political Consequences of 1992 for the European Community*, Washington DC, 1992.

Lehmbruch, Gerhard: 'Liberal Corporatism and Party Government', *Comparative Political Studies*, No. 10, 1977.

Lehmbruch, Gerhard and Schmitter, Philip (eds.): *Patterns of Corporatist Policy-Making*, London, 1982.

Levy, Jonah: 'After Etatisme: Dilemmas of Institutional Reform in Post-dirigiste France', final chapter in *Toqueville's Revenge: Dilemmas of Institution Building in Post-dirigiste France*, PhD Dissertation, Political Science Department, University of California, Berkeley, 1994.

Lindberg, L. and Scheingold, S.: *Europe's Would-Be Polity*, New Jersey, 1970.

List, Friedrich: *The National System of Political Economy*, London (Berlin), 1909, (1841).

Lundvall, Bengt-Åke: 'Innovation as an Interactive Process: User-Producer Relations.' in Dosi, Giovanni et. al (eds.): *Technical Change and Economic Theory*, London, 1988.

Lundvall, Bengt-Åke: *The Learning Economy – Challenges to Economic Theory and Policy*, Paper presented at EAEPE Annual Conference, Copenhagen 1994.

March, James and Olsen, Johan: *Rediscovering Institutions*, New York, 1989.

Marin, Bernd and Mayntz, Renate (eds.): *Policy Networks: Empirical Evidence and Theoretical Considerations*, Frankfurt a. M., 1991.

Maslow, Abraham H.: *Motivation and Personality*, New York, 1954.

Mclaughlin, D.: 'The Involvement of the Social Partners at the European Level.', in Vandamme, J.: *New Dimensions in European Social Policy*, Croom Helm, 1985.

Meehan, Elizabeth: *Citizenship and the European Community*, London, 1993.

Meek, R.L.: *Economics and Ideology and Other Essays*, London, Chapman & Hall, 1967.

Miliband, Ralph: *Class Power and State Power*, London, 1983.

Molle, Willem: *The Economics of European Integration – Theory, Practice, Policy*, Aldershot, 1990.

Monggaard, Dorte: 'Ny europæisk overenskomst', *LO-Bladet*, No. 25, 1990.

Moravcsik, Andrew: 'Preferences and Power in the European Community: A Liberal Intergovernmentalist Approach' in *Journal of Common Market Studies*, Vol. 31. No. 4, December 1993.

Morettini: Yves: 'Advisory Committee on Safety, Hygiene and Health Protection at Work' in *Social Europe*, 1990.

Neumann, Iver B. (ed.): *The 'English School' of International Relations: A Conference Report*, Oslo, 1994.

Nielsen, Ruth and Szyszczak, Erika: *The Social Dimension of the European Community*, Copenhagen, 1991.

Nugent, Neill: *The Governments and Politics of the European Communities*, London, 1990.

Nye, Joseph S.: *Peace in Parts*, Boston, 1987.

Obst, Wolfgang: 'The Safety and Health Commission for the Mining and

Other Extractive Industries: a Double Role', in *Social Europe*, 1990.

Pedersen, Ove K.: *Learning Processes and the Game of Negotiation*, Copenhagen (COS Research Report 12/1990), 1990.

Pentland, Charles: *International Theory and European Integration*, New York, 1974.

Plaschke, Henrik: *A Political Economy Approach to Regional Integration*, paper presented at CEPE, Lille, 1995.

Polanyi, Karl: *The Great Transformation*, Boston, 1957 (1944).

Pollard, Sidney: *The Integration of the European Economy since 1815*, London, 1981.

Porter, Michael: *The Competitive Advantage of Nations*, New York, 1990.

Poulantzas, Nico: *State, Power, Socialism*, London, 1978.

Rokkan, Stein: 'Electoral Mobilization, Party Competition and National Integration' in LaPalombara, Joseph and Weiner, Myron (eds): *Political Parties and Political Development*, Princeton University Press, 1966.

Rokkan, Stein: 'Norway: Numerical Democracy and Corporate Pluralism' in Dahl, Robert A. (ed.): *Political Oppositions in Western Democracies*, New Haven: Yale University Press, 1966.

Ross, George: *Jacques Delors and European Integration*, Cambridge, 1995.

Sable, C. and Piore, M.: *The Second Industrial Divide*, London, 1984.

Samuelson, Paul A.: *Economics: An Introductory Analysis*, New York, 1969.

Savoini, Carlo: 'The Social Dialogue in the Community', *Social Europe* No. 2, 1984.

Schmitter, Philippe: 'Still the Century of Corporatism' in *Review of Politics*, Vol. 36, 1974.

Schmitter, Philippe: 'Corporatisme and the State' in Grant, Wyn and Sargent, Jane (eds.): *The Political Economy of Neo-corporatism*, London, 1985.

Schumpeter, Joseph A.: *Capitalism, Socialism and Socialdemocracy*, New York, 1946.

Shonfield, Andrew: *Modern Capitalism*, Oxford, 1965.

Skocpol, Thedda: *States and Social Revolutions*, Cambridge, 1979.

Smith, Martin J.: 'Pluralism, Reformed Pluralism and Neopluralism: the Role of Pressure Groups in Policy-Making', *Political Studies*, Vol. XXXVIII, 1990.

Soskice, David: *The Institutional Infrastructures for International Competitiveness: A Comparative Analysis of the UK and Germany*, Unpublished paper (Berlin), 1991.

Staedelin, François: 'Social Policy, Social Charter, Basic Rights' in *Social Europe*, No. 1, 1990.

Streeck, W. and Schmitter, Philip C.: 'From National Corporatism to Transnational Pluralism' in *Politics and Society*, No. 2, 1991.

Streeck, W.: *Social Institutions and Economic Performance: Studies of Industrial Relations in Advanced Capitalist Economies*, London, 1992.

Subramaniam, V.: 'Representative Bureaucracy: A Reassessment' in *American Political Science Review*, Vol. 61, No. 4, 1967.

Swedeberg, R.: *Joseph A. Schumpeter – His Life and Work*, Cambridge, 1991.

Sweeney, Jane P.: *The First European Elections*, Washington, 1980.

Teague, Paul and Grahl, John: 'The European Community Social Charter and Labour Market Regulation' in *Journal of Public Policies*, No. 2, 1992.

Tönnies, Ferdinand: *Fundamental Concepts of Sociology: Gemeinschaft and Geselschaft*, New York, 1940.

Tromborg, Per: *Den Sociale Dimension*, Unpublished paper, University of Roskilde, 1991.

Urwin, Derek, W.: *The Community of Europe*, Harlow, Essex, 1991.

Venturini, Patrick: *1992 – det sociale perspektiv*, Luxembourg, 1989.

Vincent, John R.: *Human Rights and International Relations*, Cambridge, 1986.

Wallace, William, and Wallace, Helen and Webb, Carole (eds.): *Policy-Making in the European Community*, London, 1976.

Weiss, M.: 'The Industrial Relations of Occupational Health: The Impact of the Framework Directive on the Federal Republic of Germany' in *The International Journal of Comparative Labour Law and Industrial Relations*, No. 6, 1990.

Williamson, Peter J.: *Varieties of Corporatism*, Cambridge, 1985.

Williamson, Peter J.: *Corporatism in Perspective*, London, 1989.

Windmuller, John P. (et. al): *Collective Bargaining in Industrialized Economies: A Reappraisal*, Geneva, 1987.

Zysman, John: *Governments, Markets and Growth*, Oxford, 1983.

# Index